Taste of Home

BRUNCH CLASSICS

TASTE OF HOME BOOKS • RDA ENTHUSIAST BRANDS, LLC • MILWAUKEE, WI

Taste of Home

© 2021 RDA Enthusiast Brands, LLC.
1610 N. 2nd St., Suite 102, Milwaukee WI 53212-3906
All rights reserved. Taste of Home is a registered
trademark of RDA Enthusiast Brands, LLC.
Visit us at tasteofhome.com for other Taste of Home
books and products.

ISBN: 978-1-62145-742-8
LOCC: 2021936679
Component Number: 116700106H

Executive Editor: Mark Hagen
Senior Art Director: Raeann Thompson
Art Director: Maggie Conners
Deputy Editor, Copy Desk: Dulcie Shoener
Copy Editor: Kara Dennison
Contributing Editor: Michelle Rozumalski
Contributing Designer: Jen Ruetz

Cover Photographer: Jim Wieland
Cover Set Stylist: Stacey Genaw
Cover Food Stylist: Josh Rink

Pictured on front cover:
Veggie-Packed Strata, p. 35
Rhubarb Lemonade Slush, p. 7
Overnight Yeast Waffles, p. 97

Pictured on title page:
Chicken Potpie Galette with
Cheddar-Thyme Crust, p. 63

Pictured on back cover:
Easter Egg Bread, p. 89
Chocolate Lover's Pancakes, p. 98
Fruity Croissant Puff, p. 58

Printed in USA
1 3 5 7 9 10 8 6 4 2

**MORE WAYS TO
CONNECT WITH US:**

TABLE OF CONTENTS

It's Time for Brunch!

POP THE BUBBLY, TOAST THE BAGELS AND GET READY FOR YOUR BEST SUNDAY FUNDAY EVER.

What's the greatest thing to happen all week? Many people would say it's brunch—the delicious matinee event that lets you celebrate without the cost or pressure of a formal dinner party.

With *Taste of Home Brunch Classics,* you can create the best brunch ever, in the comfort of your home! Inside, you will discover so many incredible recipes—from mimosas and flavored coffee to make-ahead egg bakes and sweet morning pastries—all perfect for a.m. feasts.

The impressive eye-openers found here come together quicker than you'd imagine and include everyone's all-time favorites, such as indulgent French toast, dressed-up pancakes and new takes on bacon. You'll even find brunchworthy sandwiches, delightful smoothies, and the tangy jams and jellies everyone adores.

In addition, three at-a-glance icons spotlight dishes that make mornings merry:

MAKE AHEAD Overnight and freezer-friendly recipes you can prepare in advance

🕐 Fast-to-fix dishes ready to enjoy in 30 minutes or less

5i Five-ingredient specialties that require only a handful of items (not including water, salt, pepper, oil or optional garnishes)

Best of all, five complete menus make it a snap to host the perfect early get-together. Plan an ideal Easter meal, serve a pancake and waffle buffet, welcome Christmas morning in style, and make other morning gatherings extra special with these impressive brunch plans.

Bring the corner bistro into your home with 200+ recipes, hostess tips, how-to photos, menu ideas and so much more. Whether your gathering is casual or formal, let *Taste of Home Brunch Classics* make your morning celebrations sunny and bright.

ay tomato

say...

dy Mary

Drinks to Clink

Blend, brew, chill, ice and shake your
way to the perfect morning bevvy.
Get your sparkle on.

BELMONT BREEZE

Here's the perfect cocktail for whiskey lovers to sip on a warm afternoon. The sunny drink is juicy but not too sweet.

—*Taste of Home* Test Kitchen

TAKES: 5 MIN. • **MAKES:** 1 SERVING

- ½ to ¾ cup ice cubes
- 1½ oz. whiskey
- 1½ oz. orange juice
- 1½ oz. cranberry juice
- 1 oz. sour mix
- ¾ oz. sherry
- 1 oz. club soda
- 1 oz. lemon-lime soda
  Mint sprig and lemon wedge

1. Fill a shaker three-fourths full with ice. Place remaining ice in a cocktail glass; set aside.
2. Add the whiskey, juices, sour mix and sherry to shaker; cover and shake for 10-15 seconds or until condensation forms on outside of shaker. Strain into prepared glass. Top with sodas. Garnish with mint and lemon wedge.

1 serving: 223 cal., 0 fat (0 sat. fat),0 chol., 13mg sod., 29g carb. (27g sugars, 0 fiber), 0 pro.

STRAWBERRY BANANA YOGURT SMOOTHIE

Frozen berries and banana make my frosty smoothie extra thick and satisfying. It blends together in just 5 minutes and kicks off the day in a nutritious way.

—Christy Adkins, Martinez, GA

TAKES: 5 MIN. • **MAKES:** 2 SERVINGS

- ½ cup 2% milk
- ⅓ cup strawberry yogurt
- ⅓ cup frozen unsweetened strawberries
- ½ medium firm banana, chopped
- 4 ice cubes
- 8 tsp. sugar

In a blender, combine all of the ingredients; cover and process for 30-45 seconds or until smooth. Stir if necessary. Pour into 2 chilled glasses; serve immediately.

1 cup: 171 cal., 2g fat (1g sat. fat), 7mg chol., 52mg sod., 36g carb. (32g sugars, 1g fiber), 4g pro.

RHUBARB LEMONADE SLUSH

MAKE AHEAD

RHUBARB LEMONADE SLUSH

My family's big on rhubarb, but even people who aren't crazy about it enjoy this vodka lemonade slush. It's nice to have in the freezer for unexpected guests.

—Cathie Beard, Philomath, OR

PREP: 30 MIN. + FREEZING
MAKES: 12 SERVINGS

- 3 cups chopped fresh or frozen rhubarb
- 1 cup water
- ⅓ cup sugar
- 1 cup vodka
- ¾ cup thawed pink lemonade concentrate
- 1 bottle (2 liters) lemon-lime soda, chilled

1. In a large saucepan, bring rhubarb, water and sugar to a boil. Reduce heat, simmer, covered, 5 minutes or until rhubarb is tender. Cool slightly.
2. Puree mixture in a blender; transfer to a 1-qt. freezer container. Stir in vodka and lemonade concentrate. Freeze, covered, until firm, at least 8 hours.
3. To serve, transfer mixture to a pitcher; stir in soda. Or, for each serving, place ⅓ cup rhubarb mixture in an 8-oz. glass; stir in ⅔ cup soda.

1 cup: 180 cal., 0 fat (0 sat. fat), 0 chol., 19mg sod., 35g carb.(31g sugars, 1g fiber), 0 pro.

LEMON-BASIL MOJITO MOCKTAILS

Classic mojitos get a refreshing twist when you replace the mint with lemon and basil. This version is nonalcoholic—feel free to add your favorite rum or vodka.
—Cheryl Perry, Hertford, NC

PREP: 15 MIN. + CHILLING
MAKES: 12 SERVINGS

1½ cups sugar
  4 cups water
  6 cups fresh basil leaves, divided
     Crushed ice, divided
  2 bottles (1 liter each) club soda
GARNISH
     Fresh lemon wedges

1. In a small saucepan, bring sugar and water to a boil. Cook and stir until sugar is dissolved. Place half of the basil leaves in a small bowl. With a pestle or wooden spoon, crush the basil until its aroma is released. Stir into the sugar mixture. Remove from heat; cool completely. Strain; refrigerate until cold.
2. Place 2 cups crushed ice and the remaining basil in a 4-qt. pitcher. Using a muddler or a wooden spoon, press basil leaves against ice until their aroma is released. Stir in basil syrup and soda. Serve over crushed ice in tall glasses; squeeze lemon wedges into drink.
1 serving: 101 cal., 0 fat (0 sat. fat), 0 chol., 36mg sod., 26g carb. (25g sugars, 0 fiber), 0 pro.

BLUEBERRY PANCAKE SMOOTHIE

BLUEBERRY PANCAKE SMOOTHIE

Have your pancakes and drink them, too! A smoothie brimming with fruit, oatmeal, maple syrup and cinnamon is wonderful in the morning or any time of day. If your blueberries are fresh instead of frozen, freeze the banana ahead of time.
—Kailey Thompson, Palm Bay, FL

TAKES: 5 MIN. • **MAKES:** 2 SERVINGS

  1 cup unsweetened almond milk
  1 medium banana
½ cup frozen unsweetened blueberries
¼ cup instant plain oatmeal
  1 tsp. maple syrup
½ tsp. ground cinnamon
     Dash sea salt

Place the first 6 ingredients in a blender; cover and process until smooth. Pour the mixture into 2 chilled glasses; sprinkle with sea salt. Serve immediately.
1 cup: 153 cal., 3g fat (0 sat. fat), 0 chol., 191mg sod., 31g carb. (13g sugars, 5g fiber), 3g pro.
Diabetic exchanges: 2 starch.

LEMON-BASIL MOJITO MOCKTAILS

Uncle Merle's Bloody Mary

Bloody Mary Bar
1. FILL WITH ICE
2. SPLASH IN THE GOOD STUFF
3. SKEWER GARNISH
4. ENJOY!

You say tomato I say... Bloody Mary

UNCLE MERLE'S BLOODY MARY

A very good friend of mine was known to everyone—even people who weren't his relatives—as Uncle Merle. He gave me this recipe and made me promise not to share it until he passed away. Now Uncle Merle is gone, but his amazing cocktail lives on.
—Ronald Roth, Three Rivers, MI

TAKES: 10 MIN. • **MAKES:** 5 SERVINGS

- 4 cups tomato juice
- 1 Tbsp. white vinegar
- 1½ tsp. sugar
- 1½ tsp. Worcestershire sauce
- 1 tsp. beef bouillon granules
- ½ tsp. salt
- ¼ tsp. onion powder
- ¼ tsp. celery salt
- ¼ tsp. pepper
- ⅛ tsp. garlic powder
- 1 drop hot pepper sauce
  Dash ground cinnamon, optional
  Ice cubes
- 7½ oz. vodka

Optional garnishes: Celery ribs, cooked shrimp, cherry tomatoes, jalapeno peppers, string cheese, lemon wedges, cooked bacon, beef snack sticks, cucumber spears, olives, cubed cheese, Old Bay Seasoning and celery salt

In a pitcher, mix the first 11 ingredients until blended. If desired, stir in cinnamon. For each serving, pour ¾ cup mixture over ice; stir in 1½ Tbsp. of vodka. Garnish as desired.
1 cup: 119 cal., 1g fat (0 sat. fat), 0 chol., 961mg sod., 9g carb. (7g sugars, 1g fiber), 2g pro.

BRIGHT IDEA

DIY Bloody Mary Bar

For decorative rims, wipe each rim with a lemon wedge, then dip into a mixture of coarse salt, smoked paprika, seafood seasoning and/or celery salt. Also, set out bowls of fixings so guests can create their own masterpiece. Add beer chasers if desired.

ORANGE DREAM MIMOSAS

Bring back sweet memories with this grown-up Creamsicle in a glass. For the kiddos, make a nonalcoholic version using sparkling cider, grape juice or ginger ale in place of the champagne.
—Deirdre Cox, Kansas City, MO

PREP: 15 MIN. + FREEZING
MAKES: 16 SERVINGS (4 CUPS FROZEN MIX)

- 4 tsp. grated orange zest
- 2½ cups orange juice
- 1 cup half-and-half cream
- ¾ cup superfine sugar
- 2 bottles (750 ml each) champagne or other sparkling wine
  Fresh strawberries

1. Place the first 4 ingredients in a blender; cover and process until the sugar is dissolved. Transfer to an 8-in. square dish; freeze, covered, 6 hours or overnight.
2. To serve, place ¼ cup orange mixture in each champagne glass. Top with the champagne. Garnish with strawberries; serve immediately.

1 serving: 138 cal., 2g fat (1g sat. fat), 8mg chol., 8mg sod., 15g carb. (13g sugars, 0 fiber), 1g pro.

ORANGE DREAM MIMOSA MOCKTAILS: Substitute 2 bottles (750 ml each) sparkling apple cider for the champagne.

BLACK-EYED SUSAN

ORANGE DREAM MIMOSAS

BLACK-EYED SUSAN

The Kentucky Derby has the mint julep; the Preakness has the black-eyed Susan. It's a sunny mix of vodka, rum, and orange and pineapple juices—the perfect way to add extra cheer to gatherings.
—*Taste of Home* Test Kitchen

TAKES: 5 MIN. • **MAKES:** 1 SERVING

- ½ to ¾ cup crushed ice
- 1 oz. vodka
- 1 oz. light rum
- ½ oz. Triple Sec
- 2 oz. unsweetened pineapple juice
- 2 oz. orange juice
  Lime slice and pitted sweet dark cherry

Place desired amount of ice in a rocks glass. Pour vodka, rum, Triple Sec and juices into glass. Stir; serve with a lime slice and cherry.

1 serving: 242 cal., 0 fat (0 sat. fat), 0 chol., 3mg sod., 21g carb. (18g sugars, 0 fiber), 0 pro.

RAINBOW SPRITZER

Colorful fruit brightens up this bubbly delight. It's almost too pretty to drink!
—Olivia Thompson, Milwaukee, WI

TAKES: 20 MIN. • **MAKES:** 4 SERVINGS

- ½ cup fresh blueberries
- ½ cup chopped peeled kiwifruit
- ½ cup chopped fresh pineapple
- ½ cup sliced fresh strawberries or fresh raspberries
- 1 cup chilled ginger ale
- ½ cup chilled unsweetened pineapple juice
- ½ cup chilled lemonade

In 4 tall glasses, layer blueberries, kiwi, pineapple and strawberries. In a 2-cup glass measure or small pitcher, mix remaining ingredients; pour over fruit. Serve immediately.

1 serving: 91 cal., 0 fat (0 sat. fat), 0 chol., 8mg sod., 23g carb. (18g sugars, 2g fiber), 1g pro.

COCONUT COLD-BREW LATTE

COCONUT COLD-BREW LATTE

Cold-brew lattes are a coffeehouse favorite, but it's so easy to make them at home, too. My go-to recipe? A coconut version that's ridiculously refreshing—and vegan!
—Natalie Larsen, Columbia, MD

PREP: 20 MIN. + CHILLING
MAKES: 4 SERVINGS

- ½ cup coarsely ground medium-roast coffee
- ½ cup hot water (205°)
- 3½ cups cold water

COCONUT SIMPLE SYRUP
- 1 cup water
- ½ cup sugar
- ½ cup sweetened shredded coconut

EACH SERVING
- Ice cubes
- 2 Tbsp. coconut milk

1. Place coffee grounds in a clean glass container. Pour hot water over grounds; let stand 10 minutes. Stir in cold water. Cover and refrigerate for 12-24 hours. (The longer the coffee sits, the stronger the flavor.)
2. Meanwhile, for coconut simple syrup, in a small saucepan, bring the water, sugar and coconut to a boil. Reduce heat; simmer 10 minutes. Strain and discard the coconut. Cool completely.
3. Strain the coffee through a fine mesh sieve; discard the grounds. Strain coffee again through a coffee filter; discard the grounds. Store coffee in the refrigerator for up to 2 weeks. For each serving, fill a large glass with ice. Add 1 cup cold brewed coffee and 4 Tbsp. coconut syrup; stir. Top with coconut milk.

1 cup: 145 cal., 5g fat (5g sat. fat), 0 chol., 12mg sod., 26g carb. (26g sugars, 0 fiber), 1g pro.

RAINBOW SPRITZER

Brunch Bites

Go ahead and invite the gang.
These mix-and-match dishes make
for good morning grazing.

CAPRESE SALAD KABOBS

Bring a taste of Italy to your table with simply elegant skewers. They're great for events but so easy to assemble that I often set out a platter just for my family to snack on.
—Christine Mitchell, Glendora, CA

TAKES: 10 MIN. • **MAKES:** 12 KABOBS

- 24 grape tomatoes
- 12 cherry-size fresh mozzarella cheese balls
- 24 fresh basil leaves
- 2 Tbsp. olive oil
- 2 tsp. balsamic vinegar

On each of 12 appetizer skewers, alternately thread 2 tomatoes, 1 cheese ball and 2 basil leaves. Whisk the olive oil and vinegar; drizzle over kabobs.

1 kabob: 44 cal., 4g fat (1g sat. fat), 5mg chol., 10mg sod., 2g carb. (1g sugars, 0 fiber), 1g pro.
Diabetic exchanges: 1 fat.

READER REVIEW
"I served these at a wedding I catered, and everyone loved them. I couldn't find fresh basil leaves in the quantity I needed at a price the bride could afford, so I substituted chopped fresh basil. I just mixed it with the oil and vinegar and marinated the cheese balls, then brushed more of the mixture over the kabobs before serving."
—FAITHANDCHOCOLATE, TASTEOFHOME.COM

TOMATO-GOAT CHEESE SPREAD

A good friend shared this special recipe with me. I knew right away it was a keeper! I think the cheese spread pairs best with crackers that aren't strongly seasoned.
—Linda Alexander, Madison, WI

TAKES: 10 MIN. • **MAKES:** 12 SERVINGS

- 1 jar (8½ oz.) julienned oil-packed sun-dried tomatoes
- 2 garlic cloves, minced
- 1 log (11 oz.) fresh goat cheese
  Minced fresh parsley, optional
  Assorted crackers

1. Drain sun-dried tomatoes, reserving 3 Tbsp. of oil.
2. In a small skillet, heat the reserved oil, tomatoes and garlic over medium-high heat. Cook and stir 5 minutes or until the garlic is golden and the tomatoes are heated through. To serve, place the goat cheese on a serving plate. Pour tomato mixture over cheese. If desired, sprinkle with parsley. Serve with crackers.
1 serving: 117 cal., 9g fat (3g sat. fat), 17mg chol., 158mg sod., 6g carb. (0 sugars, 1g fiber), 4g pro.

CAPRESE SALAD KABOBS

**COASTAL CAROLINA
MUFFIN-TIN FRITTATAS**

LAYERED HUMMUS DIP

*My love for Greece inspired me to create
a quick-to-fix Mediterranean dip. I make
it for parties and any time I have a craving
for garden-fresh veggies.*
—Cheryl Snavely, Hagerstown, MD

TAKES: 15 MIN. • **MAKES:** 12 SERVINGS

- 1 carton (10 oz.) hummus
- ¼ cup finely chopped red onion
- ½ cup Greek olives, chopped
- 2 medium tomatoes, seeded
  and chopped
- 1 large English cucumber, chopped
- 1 cup crumbled feta cheese
  Baked pita chips

Spread the hummus into a shallow
10-in. round dish. Layer with onion,
olives, tomatoes, cucumber and feta.
Refrigerate until serving. Serve with
pita chips.
1 serving: 88 cal., 5g fat (2g sat. fat), 5mg
chol., 275mg sod., 6g carb. (1g sugars,
2g fiber), 4g pro.
Diabetic exchanges: 1 fat, ½ starch.

COASTAL CAROLINA MUFFIN-TIN FRITTATAS

*Loaded with the flavors of a South Carolina
low country crab boil, these mini frittatas
from a muffin pan are deliciously satisfying.
Have leftover roasted or boiled potatoes in
the fridge? Feel free to dice them and use
them in place of the hash browns.*
—Shannon Kohn, Summerville, SC

PREP: 30 MIN. • **BAKE:** 30 MIN.
MAKES: 1 DOZEN

- ½ cup mayonnaise
- 1 Tbsp. lemon juice
- 2 tsp. sugar
- 1 tsp. seafood seasoning
- 2 cups refrigerated shredded
  hash brown potatoes
- 1½ cups chopped smoked sausage
- 1 can (8 oz.) jumbo lump crabmeat,
  drained
- ¼ cup chopped roasted sweet
  red peppers
- 7 large eggs
- ¾ cup heavy whipping cream
- 1 Tbsp. Louisiana-style hot sauce
- ½ tsp. salt
- 12 bacon strips, cooked and crumbled
- ¼ cup thinly sliced green onions

1. Preheat oven to 350°. In a small bowl,
combine mayonnaise, lemon juice, sugar
and seafood seasoning. Refrigerate the
mixture until serving.
2. Meanwhile, in a large bowl, combine
the potatoes, sausage, crab and red
peppers. Divide among 12 greased
jumbo muffin cups. In another large
bowl, whisk the eggs, cream, hot sauce
and salt. Pour over the potato mixture.
Top with bacon.
3. Bake 30-35 minutes or until a knife
inserted in center comes out clean.
Serve with sauce and green onions.
1 frittata: 292 cal., 23g fat (8g sat. fat),
164mg chol., 768mg sod., 7g carb. (2g
sugars, 1g fiber), 13g pro.

BOURBON CANDIED BACON DEVILED EGGS

PULLED PORK DOUGHNUT HOLE SLIDERS

When we had root beer pulled pork left over from a party, we started experimenting, and these sliders were born. Now we don't want barbecue any other way!
—Eden Dranger, Los Angeles, CA

PREP: 55 MIN. • **COOK:** 8 HOURS
MAKES: 5 DOZEN

- 1 bottle (2 liters) root beer
- 1½ cups barbecue sauce
- 1½ tsp. salt
- 1 tsp. minced fresh gingerroot
- 1 bone-in pork shoulder roast (about 3 lbs.)

SLAW
- ½ cup mayonnaise or Miracle Whip
- 2 Tbsp. white vinegar
- 1 Tbsp. maple syrup
- 1 pkg. (14 oz.) coleslaw mix

ASSEMBLY
- 60 plain doughnut holes
- 60 appetizer skewers
  Additional barbecue sauce, optional

1. In a large saucepan, bring root beer to a boil. Reduce heat to medium-high; cook, uncovered, until liquid is reduced by half, 30-45 minutes. Transfer to a 5- or 6-qt. slow cooker. Stir in barbecue sauce, salt and ginger. Add roast, turning to coat.
2. Cook, covered, on low until the pork is tender, 8-10 hours. For slaw, in a large bowl, mix the mayonnaise, vinegar and syrup. Stir in coleslaw mix. Refrigerate, covered, until the flavors are blended, at least 1 hour.
3. Remove the pork from slow cooker; skim fat from cooking juices. Remove meat from bones; shred with 2 forks. Return juices and pork to slow cooker; heat through.
4. To serve, cut doughnut holes in half; cut a thin slice off the bottoms to level. Serve pork and slaw in doughnut holes; secure with skewers. If desired, serve with additional barbecue sauce.
Freeze option: Freeze the cooled pork mixture in freezer containers. To use, partially thaw in refrigerator overnight. Heat through in a covered saucepan, stirring gently.
1 slider: 138 cal., 7g fat (2g sat. fat), 13mg chol., 218mg sod., 14g carb. (10g sugars, 0 fiber), 5g pro.

BOURBON CANDIED BACON DEVILED EGGS

In our house, it doesn't get any better than deviled eggs with bacon—bourbon candied bacon, that is. See if you can resist them. We can't!
—Colleen Delawder, Herndon, VA

PREP: 20 MIN. • **BAKE:** 25 MIN.
MAKES: 2 DOZEN

- 2 Tbsp. brown sugar
- ¾ tsp. Dijon mustard
- ½ tsp. maple syrup
- ⅛ tsp. salt
- 2 tsp. bourbon, optional
- 4 thick-sliced bacon strips

EGGS
- 12 hard-boiled large eggs
- ¾ cup mayonnaise
- 1 Tbsp. maple syrup
- 1 Tbsp. Dijon mustard
- ¼ tsp. pepper
- ¼ tsp. ground chipotle pepper
  Minced fresh chives

1. Preheat oven to 350°. In a small bowl, mix brown sugar, ¾ tsp. mustard, ½ tsp. syrup and salt. If desired, stir in bourbon. Coat bacon with brown sugar mixture. Place on a rack in a foil-lined 15x10x1-in. baking pan. Bake 25-30 minutes or until crisp. Cool completely.
2. Cut eggs in half lengthwise. Remove yolks, reserving whites. In a small bowl, mash yolks. Add mayonnaise, 1 Tbsp. syrup, 1 Tbsp. mustard and both types of pepper; stir until smooth. Chop bacon finely; fold half into the egg yolk mixture. Spoon or pipe into egg whites. Sprinkle with remaining bacon and the chives. Refrigerate, covered, until serving.
1 stuffed egg half: 107 cal., 9g fat (2g sat. fat), 97mg chol., 142mg sod., 2g carb. (2g sugars, 0 fiber), 4g pro.

PULLED PORK
DOUGHNUT
HOLE SLIDERS

BANANAS FOSTER CRUNCH MIX

Bananas Foster is one of my favorite desserts. I came up with another way to enjoy it—a crunchy, snackable version eaten by the handful. The sweet mix is fun to pack in bags and give as gifts, too.
—David Dahlman, Chatsworth, CA

PREP: 10 MIN. • **COOK:** 5 MIN. + COOLING
MAKES: 2½ QT.

- 3 cups Honey Nut Chex
- 3 cups Cinnamon Chex
- 2¼ cups pecan halves
- 1½ cups dried banana chips
- ⅓ cup butter, cubed
- ⅓ cup packed brown sugar
- ½ tsp. ground cinnamon
- ½ tsp. banana extract
- ½ tsp. rum extract

1. Place the first 4 ingredients in a large microwave-safe bowl. Place the butter, brown sugar and cinnamon in a small microwave-safe bowl; microwave on high for 2 minutes, stirring once. Stir in extracts. Pour over cereal mixture; toss to coat.
2. Microwave cereal mixture on high for 3 minutes, stirring every minute. Spread onto baking sheets to cool. Store in an airtight container.

¾ cup: 358 cal., 24g fat (9g sat. fat), 14mg chol., 170mg sod., 36g carb. (18g sugars, 4g fiber), 4g pro.

CHOCOLATE FRUIT DIP

CHOCOLATE FRUIT DIP

Guests just keep coming back for more of this tempting treat. I usually choose strawberries and pineapple chunks as dippers, but it's yummy with other fruits as well. Try apples, melon or grapes.
—Sarah Maury Swan, Granite, MD

TAKES: 10 MIN. • **MAKES:** 2 CUPS

- 1 pkg. (8 oz.) cream cheese, softened
- ⅓ cup sugar
- ⅓ cup baking cocoa
- 1 tsp. vanilla extract
- 2 cups whipped topping
  Assorted fruit for dipping

In a large bowl, beat cream cheese and sugar until smooth. Beat in cocoa and vanilla. Beat in whipped topping until smooth. Serve with fresh fruit.

2 Tbsp.: 96 cal., 7g fat (5g sat. fat), 16mg chol., 42mg sod., 8g carb. (5g sugars, 0 fiber), 1g pro.

READER REVIEW
"Not only would I make this recipe again, I've already made it time and again. I'm getting ready to prepare three more batches to serve at a friend's recital reception. The dip is rich and decadent, yet light and airy, like a mousse. I personally like strawberries best for dipping."
— RECIPEME579, TASTEOFHOME.COM

BAGEL WITH A VEGGIE SCHMEAR

I got this recipe from a popular bagel shop in New York City. Sometimes I toss chopped pitted green olives into the schmear. Either way, it adds up to a fast, flavorful bite.
—Julie Merriman, Seattle, WA

TAKES: 20 MIN. • **MAKES:** 4 SERVINGS

- 4 oz. fat-free cream cheese
- 4 oz. fresh goat cheese
- ½ tsp. grated lime zest
- 1 Tbsp. lime juice
- ⅔ cup finely chopped cucumber
- ¼ cup finely chopped celery
- 3 Tbsp. finely chopped carrot
- 1 radish, finely chopped
- 2 Tbsp. finely chopped red onion
- 2 Tbsp. thinly sliced fresh basil
- 4 whole wheat bagels, split and toasted
- 8 slices tomato
  Coarsely ground pepper, optional

In a bowl, beat cheeses, lime zest and lime juice until blended. Fold in chopped vegetables and basil. Serve on bagels with tomato slices. If desired, sprinkle with pepper.

2 open-faced sandwiches: 341 cal., 6g fat (3g sat. fat), 22mg chol., 756mg sod., 56g carb. (15g sugars, 10g fiber), 20g pro.

HOW-TO

Cut Bagels for Low Commitment

Order bagels uncut so you can thinly slice them vertically at home. This makes for easy sampling.

MAKE AHEAD

HAM & BRIE PASTRIES

Growing up, I loved pocket pastries. Now with a busy family, I need quick bites that satisfy everyone. My little ham-and-cheese bundles go over big as a snack and even a light dinner.
—Jenn Tidwell, Fair Oaks, CA

TAKES: 30 MIN. • **MAKES:** 16 PASTRIES

- 1 sheet frozen puff pastry, thawed
- ⅓ cup apricot preserves
- 4 slices deli ham, quartered
- 8 oz. Brie cheese, cut into 16 pieces

1. Preheat oven to 400°. On a lightly floured surface, unfold puff pastry. Roll pastry to a 12-in. square; cut into sixteen 3-in. squares. Place 1 tsp. of preserves in center of each square; top with deli ham, folding as necessary, and cheese. Overlap 2 opposite corners of each pastry over filling; pinch tightly to seal.
2. Place on a parchment-lined baking sheet. Bake 15-20 minutes or until golden brown. Cool on the pan for 5 minutes before serving.
Freeze option: Freeze cooled pastries in a freezer container, separating the layers with waxed paper. To use, reheat frozen pastries on a baking sheet in a preheated 400° oven until heated through.
1 appetizer: 144 cal., 8g fat (3g sat. fat), 17mg chol., 192mg sod., 13g carb. (3g sugars, 1g fiber), 5g pro.

BAGEL WITH A VEGGIE SCHMEAR

Pancakes & Waffles

Got a sweet spot for crepes, French toast or other lazy-day favorites? Brunch is the time to settle in and enjoy!

APPLE PIE RICOTTA WAFFLES

When I had extra apples and ricotta cheese to use up, I decided to try something new. The result was a fluffy, tender waffle with just a hint of sweetness.

—Teri Rasey, Cadillac, MI

PREP: 25 MIN. • **COOK:** 10 MIN./BATCH
MAKES: 6 SERVINGS

- ¼ cup butter
- 6 medium apples, peeled and chopped
- 2 Tbsp. sugar
- 1 Tbsp. honey
- 1 tsp. ground cinnamon
- 1 tsp. vanilla extract

WAFFLES
- 2 cups all-purpose flour
- 2 Tbsp. quick-cooking grits
- 1 Tbsp. cornstarch
- 1 tsp. baking soda
- ½ tsp. salt
- 2 large eggs, room temperature
- 2 cups buttermilk
- 1 cup reduced-fat ricotta cheese
- ½ cup canola oil
- 2 tsp. vanilla extract
- 1½ cups fat-free vanilla Greek yogurt
  Fresh blueberries, optional

1. In a large skillet, melt butter over medium-high heat. Add the apples, sugar, honey, cinnamon and vanilla; cook and stir until the apples are crisp-tender, 10-12 minutes. Remove from heat and keep warm.
2. Preheat waffle iron. In a large bowl, whisk flour, grits, cornstarch, baking soda and salt. Whisk eggs, buttermilk, ricotta, oil and vanilla; add to the dry ingredients; stir just until moistened.
3. Bake the waffles according to the manufacturer's directions until golden brown. Serve with apple topping, yogurt and, if desired, blueberries.
1 waffle: 633 cal., 31g fat (8g sat. fat), 96mg chol., 709mg sod., 70g carb. (31g sugars, 4g fiber), 18g pro.

CHOCOLATE CHIP DUTCH BABY

A friend introduced me to the traditional version of a Dutch baby. I tweaked it a bit by sprinkling on a mixture of mini chocolate chips and brown sugar before baking.

—Mary Thompson, La Crosse, WI

TAKES: 30 MIN. • **MAKES:** 4 SERVINGS

- ¼ cup miniature semisweet chocolate chips
- ¼ cup packed brown sugar

DUTCH BABY
- ½ cup all-purpose flour
- 2 large eggs, room temperature
- ½ cup half-and-half cream
- ⅛ tsp. ground nutmeg
  Dash ground cinnamon
- 3 Tbsp. butter
  Optional: Maple syrup and additional butter

1. In a small bowl, combine chocolate chips and brown sugar; set aside. In a small bowl, beat flour, eggs, cream, nutmeg and cinnamon until smooth.
2. Place the butter in a 9-in. pie plate or an 8-in. cast-iron skillet. Heat in a 425° oven until melted, about 4 minutes. Pour batter into hot pie plate or skillet. Sprinkle with the chocolate chip mixture. Bake for 13-15 minutes or until top edge is golden brown. Serve immediately, with syrup and butter if desired.
1 piece: 313 cal., 17g fat (10g sat. fat), 144mg chol., 140mg sod., 33g carb. (21g sugars, 1g fiber), 6g pro.

APPLE PIE RICOTTA WAFFLES

BANANA BLUEBERRY PANCAKES

AUNT BETTY'S JELLY CREPES

My Aunt Betty made her jelly crepes for me when I was a boy. They're so easy to fix and so good, I've been eating them ever since.
—Richard Ward, Three Rivers, MI

TAKES: 20 MIN. • **MAKES:** 3 CREPES

- 2 large eggs, room temperature
- ¾ cup 2% milk
- ⅛ tsp. salt
- ½ cup all-purpose flour
  Butter, softened
  Strawberry or grape jelly
  Confectioners' sugar

In a small bowl, whisk eggs, milk and salt. Add flour; beat until smooth. Melt 1 tsp. butter in a 10-in. nonstick skillet. Pour ¼ cup batter into the center of the skillet; lift and turn pan to cover bottom. Cook until lightly browned; turn and brown the other side. Remove and keep warm. Repeat with the remaining batter, adding butter to the skillet as needed. Spread the crepes with butter and jelly; roll up. Dust with confectioners' sugar. Serve immediately.

1 crepe: 161 cal., 5g fat (2g sat. fat), 130mg chol., 172mg sod., 19g carb. (3g sugars, 1g fiber), 8g pro.

READER REVIEW

"These crepes are just like the ones I used to make for my children. I found the recipe 30 minutes ago and tried it right away. So delicious!"
—DLS5799, TASTEOFHOME.COM

MAKE AHEAD
BANANA BLUEBERRY PANCAKES

A favorite in our home, this recipe sneaks in whole wheat flour and adds nutritious fruit. My kids don't realize they're eating a healthier version of pancakes!
—Kelly Reinicke, Wisconsin Rapids, WI

PREP: 15 MIN. • **COOK:** 5 MIN./BATCH
MAKES: 14 PANCAKES

- 1 cup whole wheat flour
- ½ cup all-purpose flour
- 2 Tbsp. sugar
- 2 tsp. baking powder
- ½ tsp. salt
- 1 large egg, room temperature, lightly beaten
- 1¼ cups fat-free milk
- 3 medium ripe bananas, mashed
- 1 tsp. vanilla extract
- 1½ cups fresh or frozen blueberries
  Optional: Maple syrup and sliced bananas

1. In a large bowl, combine the flours, sugar, baking powder and salt. Combine egg, milk, bananas and vanilla; stir into dry ingredients just until moistened.
2. Pour the batter by ¼ cupfuls onto a hot griddle coated with cooking spray; sprinkle with blueberries. Turn when bubbles form on top; cook until second side is golden brown. If desired, serve pancakes with syrup and sliced bananas.

Freeze option: Freeze cooled pancakes between layers of waxed paper in a resealable freezer container. To use, place the pancakes on an ungreased baking sheet, cover with foil and reheat in a preheated 375° oven 6-10 minutes. Or, place a stack of 3 pancakes on a microwave-safe plate and microwave on high 1¼-1½ minutes or until cakes are heated through.

Note: If using frozen berries, do not thaw.

2 pancakes: 195 cal., 2g fat (0 sat. fat), 31mg chol., 317mg sod., 41g carb. (19g sugars, 4g fiber), 6g pro.

Diabetic exchanges: 1½ starch, 1 fruit.

BAKED PEACH PANCAKE

Whenever I go home, my mom likes to share this wonderful breakfast. We think it's best warm from the oven with a topping of sour cream and a side of bacon or ham.
—Nancy Wilkinson, Princeton, NJ

PREP: 10 MIN. • **BAKE:** 25 MIN.
MAKES: 6 SERVINGS

- 2 cups fresh or frozen sliced peeled peaches
- 4 tsp. sugar
- 1 tsp. lemon juice
- 3 large eggs, room temperature
- ½ cup all-purpose flour
- ½ cup 2% milk
- ½ tsp. salt
- 2 Tbsp. butter
  Ground nutmeg
  Sour cream, optional

1. In a small bowl, combine the peach slices, sugar and lemon juice; set aside. In a large bowl, beat the eggs until fluffy. Add the flour, milk and salt; beat until smooth.
2. Place butter in a 10-in. ovenproof skillet in a 400° oven for 3-5 minutes or until melted. Immediately pour the batter into hot skillet. Bake until the pancake has risen and puffed all over, 20-25 minutes.
3. Fill with peach slices and sprinkle with nutmeg. Serve immediately, with sour cream if desired.
1 piece: 149 cal., 7g fat (4g sat. fat), 105mg chol., 272mg sod., 17g carb. (8g sugars, 1g fiber), 5g pro.
Diabetic exchanges: 1 medium-fat meat, 1 fat, ½ starch, ½ fruit.

BIRTHDAY CAKE PANCAKES

BIRTHDAY CAKE PANCAKES

To make plain pancake mix extra special for my kids, I add cake mix and sprinkles. Frosting seals the deal!
—Dina Crowell, Fredericksburg, VA

PREP: 15 MIN. + STANDING
COOK: 5 MIN./BATCH
MAKES: 6 SERVINGS

- 1 cup pancake mix
- 1 cup yellow or white cake mix
- 2 large eggs, room temperature
- 1½ cups plus 1 Tbsp. 2% milk, divided
- 1 tsp. vanilla extract
- ¼ cup sprinkles
- ¾ cup vanilla frosting
  Additional sprinkles

1. Whisk the pancake mix and cake mix. In a separate bowl, whisk eggs, 1½ cups milk and vanilla until blended. Add to dry ingredients, stirring just until moistened. Let stand for 10 minutes. Fold in ¼ cup sprinkles.
2. On a lightly greased griddle over medium heat, pour batter by ¼ cupfuls to create 6 large pancakes. Cook until the bubbles on top begin to pop; turn. Cook until golden brown. Repeat, using smaller amounts of batter to create pancakes of different sizes.
3. Microwave the vanilla frosting and remaining milk, covered, on high until melted, 10-15 seconds. On each of the large pancakes, layer smaller pancakes in order of decreasing size with the smallest on top; drizzle with frosting. Top with additional sprinkles.
Freeze option: Freeze cooled pancakes between layers of waxed paper in a freezer container. To use, place pancakes on an ungreased baking sheet, cover with foil and reheat in a preheated 375° oven for 5-10 minutes. Or, place a stack of pancakes on a microwave-safe plate and microwave on high until heated through, 30-90 seconds.
1 serving: 396 cal., 12g fat (3g sat. fat), 67mg chol., 558mg sod., 65g carb. (38g sugars, 1g fiber), 7g pro.

HOW-TO

Make Fanciful Flapjacks
Put batter in a squeeze bottle to make pancakes in fun shapes. Try snowmen, caterpillars, hearts or letters to spell names.

BUTTERMILK PECAN WAFFLES

I like cooking with buttermilk and these nutty, golden waffles are my husband's favorite breakfast, so we enjoy them often. They're as easy to prepare as regular waffles, but their unique taste makes them exceptional.
—Edna Hoffman, Hebron, IN

PREP: 10 MIN. **COOK:** 5 MIN./BATCH
MAKES: 7 WAFFLES

- 2 cups all-purpose flour
- 1 Tbsp. baking powder
- 1 tsp. baking soda
- ½ tsp. salt
- 4 large eggs, room temperature
- 2 cups buttermilk
- ½ cup butter, melted
- 3 Tbsp. chopped pecans

1. In a large bowl, whisk flour, baking powder, baking soda and salt. In another bowl, whisk the eggs and buttermilk until blended. Add to dry ingredients; stir just until moistened. Stir in butter.
2. Pour about ¾ cup batter onto a lightly greased preheated waffle maker. Sprinkle with a few pecans. Bake according to manufacturer's directions until golden brown. Repeat with the remaining batter and chopped pecans.
1 waffle: 337 cal., 19g fat (10g sat. fat), 159mg chol., 762mg sod., 31g carb. (4g sugars, 1g fiber), 10g pro.

BANANA CREPES

BANANA CREPES

Here's one of my favorite treats to serve for brunch or even dessert after dinner. The tender, golden crepes always impress.
—Freda Becker, Garrettsville, OH

PREP: 20 MIN. + STANDING
COOK: 10 MIN. • **MAKES:** 12 CREPES

- 2 large eggs, room temperature
- ¾ cup 2% milk
- ½ cup all-purpose flour
- 1 Tbsp. butter, melted
- 1 Tbsp. sugar
- ⅛ tsp. salt

FILLING
- ½ cup butter, cubed
- ⅔ cup sugar
- 4 tsp. grated orange zest
- ⅔ cup orange juice
- 6 medium firm bananas, peeled and sliced
  Fresh raspberries, optional

1. In a bowl, whisk together the first 6 ingredients; let stand 20 minutes.
2. Heat a lightly greased 8-in. nonstick skillet over medium heat. Fill a ¼-cup measure halfway with batter; pour into center of pan. Quickly lift, tilt and rotate pan to coat bottom evenly. Cook crepe until top appears dry; turn over and cook until bottom is cooked, 15-20 seconds longer. Remove to a wire rack. Repeat with remaining batter, greasing pan as needed.
3. For filling, place butter, sugar, orange zest and juice in a large skillet; bring to a boil, stirring to dissolve sugar. Reduce heat to medium; add bananas to warm.
4. To serve, spoon bananas onto crepes; fold into quarters. Top with remaining filling and, if desired, raspberries.
2 filled crepes: 443 cal., 20g fat (12g sat. fat), 110mg chol., 226mg sod., 64g carb. (43g sugars, 3g fiber), 6g pro.

BRIGHT IDEA

For a lighter option, try these crepes with a filling of sliced bananas, strawberries, Greek yogurt and a sprinkling of granola for crunch.

BAKED BANANAS FOSTER FRENCH TOAST

If you like classic bananas Foster, you'll love this baked French toast. It has all the flavor of the traditional dessert.
—Laurence Nasson, Hingham, MA

PREP: 20 MIN. + CHILLING
BAKE: 35 MIN. • **MAKES:** 6 SERVINGS

- ½ cup butter, cubed
- ⅔ cup packed brown sugar
- ½ cup heavy whipping cream
- ½ tsp. ground cinnamon
- ½ tsp. ground allspice
- ¼ cup chopped pecans, optional
- 3 large bananas, sliced
- 12 slices egg bread or challah (about ¾ lb.)
- 1½ cups 2% milk
- 3 large eggs
- 1 Tbsp. sugar
- 1 tsp. vanilla extract

1. Place butter in a microwave-safe bowl; microwave, covered, until melted, 30-45 seconds. Stir in the brown sugar, whipping cream, cinnamon, allspice and, if desired, pecans. Add bananas; toss gently to coat.
2. Transfer to a greased 13x9-in. baking dish. Arrange bread over top, trimming to fit as necessary.
3. Place the remaining ingredients in a blender; process just until blended. Pour over bread. Refrigerate, covered, 8 hours or overnight.
4. Preheat oven to 375°. Remove the French toast from refrigerator while oven heats. Bake, uncovered, until a knife inserted in center comes out clean, 35-40 minutes. Let stand for 5-10 minutes. Invert to serve.
1 piece: 658 cal., 31g fat (17g sat. fat), 218mg chol., 584mg sod., 84g carb. (39g sugars, 4g fiber), 14g pro.

RASPBERRY-BANANA BREAKFAST TACOS

For a sweet take on breakfast tacos, replace the tortillas with pancakes and add a cream cheese filling. I vary the fruits and berries depending on what's in season.
—Joan Hallford, North Richland Hills, TX

PREP: 25 MIN. • **COOK:** 5 MIN./BATCH
MAKES: 4 SERVINGS

- ¾ cup all-purpose flour
- ¾ cup whole wheat flour
- 3 Tbsp. sugar
- 2 tsp. baking powder
- ¾ tsp. ground cinnamon
- ½ tsp. salt
- 1 large egg, room temperature
- 1 cup 2% milk
- 2 Tbsp. canola oil
- 1 tsp. vanilla extract
- ⅓ cup cream cheese, softened
- 3 Tbsp. vanilla yogurt
- 1 small banana, sliced
- 1 cup fresh raspberries

1. Whisk together flours, sugar, baking powder, cinnamon and salt. Combine the egg, milk, canola oil and vanilla; stir into dry ingredients just until moistened.
2. Preheat a griddle over medium heat. Lightly grease griddle. Pour batter by ½ cupfuls onto griddle; cook until the bubbles on top begin to pop and the bottoms are golden brown. Turn; cook until second side is golden brown.
3. Meanwhile, beat together the cream cheese and vanilla yogurt. Spread over the pancakes; top with banana and raspberries. Fold up.
1 taco: 429 cal., 17g fat (6g sat. fat), 71mg chol., 651mg sod., 59g carb. (19g sugars, 6g fiber), 11g pro.

BAKED BANANAS FOSTER FRENCH TOAST

Incredible Eggs

Humble, healthy eggs are the very symbol of life. Here are 11 wonderful ways to celebrate them.

LOADED TATER TOT BAKE

I keep frozen Tater Tots on hand for meals like this delicious casserole. It requires just 15 minutes of prep before baking and goes over big with guests of all ages.

—Nancy Heishman, Las Vegas, NV

PREP: 15 MIN. • **BAKE:** 35 MIN.
MAKES: 6 SERVINGS

- 1 Tbsp. canola oil
- 1 medium onion, finely chopped
- 6 oz. Canadian bacon, cut into ½-in. strips
- 4 cups frozen Tater Tots, thawed
- 6 large eggs, lightly beaten
- ½ cup reduced-fat sour cream
- ½ cup half-and-half cream
- 1 Tbsp. dried parsley flakes
- ¾ tsp. garlic powder
- ½ tsp. pepper
- 1½ cups shredded cheddar cheese

1. Preheat oven to 350°. In a large skillet, heat oil over medium heat. Add onion; cook and stir until tender, 2-3 minutes. Add the Canadian bacon; cook until lightly browned, 1-2 minutes, stirring occasionally. Remove from heat.
2. Line the bottom of a greased 11x7-in. baking dish with Tater Tots; top with the Canadian bacon mixture. In a large bowl, whisk the eggs, sour cream, cream and seasonings until blended. Stir in cheese; pour over top. Bake, uncovered, until golden brown, 35-40 minutes.
1 piece: 443 cal., 29g fat (12g sat. fat), 243mg chol., 917mg sod., 23g carb. (4g sugars, 2g fiber), 22g pro.

ITALIAN EGGS BENEDICT WITH PESTO HOLLANDAISE

My husband and I have a standing breakfast date on Saturdays. When we want something fancy, we treat ourselves to Italian-inspired eggs Benedict with pesto and prosciutto.
—Jackie Dodd, Los Angeles, CA

TAKES: 30 MIN. • **MAKES:** 4 SERVINGS

- ½ cup butter, cubed
- 1 Tbsp. prepared pesto
- 4 large egg yolks
- 2 Tbsp. water
- 1 Tbsp. lemon juice
- 2 tsp. white vinegar
- 4 large eggs
- 8 thin slices prosciutto or deli ham
- 4 fresh basil leaves
- 4 slices tomato
- 4 slices Italian bread (1 in. thick), toasted

1. In a small saucepan, melt the butter; stir in pesto. In top of a double boiler or a metal bowl over simmering water, whisk egg yolks, water and lemon juice until blended; cook until mixture is just thick enough to coat a metal spoon and the temperature reaches 160°, whisking constantly. Reduce heat to very low. Very slowly drizzle in the warm melted butter mixture, whisking constantly.
2. Transfer to a small bowl if necessary. Place the bowl in a larger bowl of warm water. Keep warm, stirring occasionally, until ready to serve. Place 2-3 in. water in a large saucepan or skillet with high sides; add vinegar. Bring to a boil; adjust heat to maintain a gentle simmer. Break cold eggs, 1 at a time, into a small bowl; holding bowl close to the surface of the water, slip each egg into water.
3. Cook, uncovered, 3-5 minutes or until whites are completely set and the yolks begin to thicken but are not hard. Using a slotted spoon, lift eggs out of water.
4. To serve, layer the prosciutto or ham, basil leaves, tomato and eggs over toast. Top with the hollandaise sauce. Serve immediately.
1 serving: 525 cal., 39g fat (19g sat. fat), 457mg chol., 1092mg sod., 24g carb. (2g sugars, 2g fiber), 21g pro.

ITALIAN EGGS BENEDICT WITH PESTO HOLLANDAISE

MIGAS BREAKFAST TACOS

Unless you grew up in the Southwest or have visited there frequently, you may never have heard of migas. But give them a try—you'll be glad you did! I think the corn tortilla strips are the key ingredient.

—Stephen Exel, Des Moines, IA

TAKES: 30 MIN. • **MAKES:** 3 SERVINGS

- ¼ cup finely chopped onion
- 1 jalapeno pepper, seeded and chopped
- 1 Tbsp. canola oil
- 2 corn tortillas (6 in.), cut into thin strips
- 4 large eggs
- ¼ tsp. salt
- ⅛ tsp. pepper
- ½ cup crumbled queso fresco or shredded Monterey Jack cheese
- ¼ cup chopped seeded tomato
- 6 flour tortillas (6 in.), warmed
  Optional toppings: Refried beans, sliced avocado, sour cream and minced fresh cilantro

1. In a large skillet, saute the onion and jalapeno pepper in oil until tender. Add the tortilla strips; cook 3 minutes longer. In a small bowl, whisk the eggs, salt and pepper. Add to skillet; cook and stir until almost set. Stir in cheese and tomato.
2. Serve in flour tortillas with toppings of your choice.
2 tacos: 424 cal., 21g fat (5g sat. fat), 295mg chol., 821mg sod., 39g carb. (2g sugars, 1g fiber), 21g pro.

MANCHEGO MUSHROOM SCRAMBLE

This savory dish takes the usual morning scramble up a few notches. The rich flavor from Manchego cheese, mushrooms and cream is so satisfying.

—Thomas Faglon, Somerset, NJ

TAKES: 25 MIN. • **MAKES:** 8 SERVINGS

- 2 Tbsp. extra virgin olive oil, divided
- ½ cup diced onion
- ½ cup diced sweet red pepper
- 2 cups thinly sliced fresh shiitake mushrooms (about 4 oz.)
- 1 tsp. prepared horseradish
- 8 large eggs, beaten
- 1 cup heavy whipping cream
- 1 cup shredded Manchego cheese
- 1 tsp. kosher salt
- 1 tsp. coarsely ground pepper

1. In a large nonstick skillet, heat 1 Tbsp. olive oil over medium heat. Add onion and red pepper; cook and stir until crisp-tender, 2-3 minutes. Add the mushrooms; cook and stir until tender, 3-4 minutes. Stir in the horseradish; cook 2 minutes more.
2. In a small bowl, whisk together the remaining ingredients and remaining olive oil. Pour into skillet; cook and stir until eggs are thickened and no liquid egg remains.
1 serving: 274 cal., 24g fat (12g sat. fat), 234mg chol., 405mg sod., 4g carb. (2g sugars, 1g fiber), 11g pro.

MANCHEGO MUSHROOM SCRAMBLE

SHIITAKE EGGS IN PUFF PASTRY

Shaped with ramekins, these pastries look amazing on the table and taste even better.
—Jamie Brown-Miller, Napa, CA

TAKES: 30 MIN. • **MAKES:** 4 SERVINGS

- 1 sheet thawed puff pastry
- 2 Tbsp. butter, divided
- 1½ cups sliced fresh shiitake mushrooms
- 1 cup fresh baby spinach
- 6 large eggs, lightly beaten
- ½ cup crumbled goat cheese
- 1 Tbsp. Sriracha chili sauce
- 4 thin slices prosciutto
- 1 Tbsp. minced fresh tarragon

1. Preheat the oven to 425°. Place four 6-oz. ramekins upside down on a baking sheet. Grease outsides of ramekins well. Cut pastry into quarters; shape each around a ramekin. Bake 14-16 minutes or until golden brown.

2. In a large skillet, melt 1 Tbsp. butter over medium-high heat. Add the sliced mushrooms; saute 2-3 minutes or until lightly browned. Stir in spinach until wilted. Remove from pan.

3. In same pan, heat remaining butter over medium heat. Pour in eggs; cook and stir until thickened and no liquid egg remains. Gently stir in goat cheese, chili sauce and mushroom mixture.

4. Carefully remove the pastries from the ramekins and place right-side up on plates. Line the bottoms and sides of pastries with prosciutto. Fill with egg mixture; sprinkle with tarragon.

1 serving: 545 cal., 35g fat (13g sat. fat), 324mg chol., 826mg sod., 39g carb. (2g sugars, 6g fiber), 21g pro.

CLASSIC EGGS BENEDICT

According to one account, traditional eggs Benedict first appeared at Delmonico's in New York. Whatever the origin of saucy poached eggs on an English muffin, I'm glad someone invented it!
—Barbara Pletzke, Herndon, VA

TAKES: 30 MIN. • **MAKES:** 8 SERVINGS

- 4 large egg yolks
- 2 Tbsp. water
- 2 Tbsp. lemon juice
- ¾ cup butter, melted
  Dash white pepper
ASSEMBLY
- 8 large eggs
- 4 English muffins
- 8 slices warm Canadian bacon
  Paprika

1. For the hollandaise sauce, in the top of a double boiler or a metal bowl over simmering water, whisk egg yolks, water and lemon juice until blended; cook until the mixture is just thick enough to coat a metal spoon and temperature reaches 160°, whisking constantly. Remove from heat. Very slowly drizzle in warm melted butter, whisking constantly. Whisk in the white pepper. Transfer to a small bowl if necessary. Place the bowl in a larger bowl of warm water. Keep warm, stirring occasionally, until ready to serve, up to 30 minutes.

2. Place 2-3 in. water in a large saucepan or skillet with high sides. Bring to a boil; adjust heat to maintain a gentle simmer. Break 1 egg into a small bowl; holding the bowl close to the surface of the water, slip the egg into water. Repeat with 3 more eggs.

3. Cook, uncovered, 2-4 minutes or until the whites are completely set and the yolks begin to thicken but are not hard. With a slotted spoon, lift the eggs out of water. Repeat with remaining 4 eggs.

4. Split and toast the English muffins; top each half with Canadian bacon, a poached egg and 2 Tbsp. sauce. Sprinkle with paprika.

1 serving: 345 cal., 26g fat (14g sat. fat), 331mg chol., 522mg sod., 15g carb. (1g sugars, 1g fiber), 13g pro.

CLASSIC EGGS
BENEDICT

MUFFIN CUP EGGS

My children have loved these ever since they were toddlers. With just three ingredients, the little cups couldn't be easier to make.
—Lisa Walder, Urbana, IL

TAKES: 30 MIN. • **MAKES:** 6 SERVINGS

- 12 thin slices deli roast beef
- 6 slices American cheese, quartered
- 12 large eggs

1. Press 1 slice of beef onto the bottom and up the sides of each greased muffin cup, forming a shell. Arrange 2 cheese pieces in each shell. Break 1 egg into each cup.
2. Bake, uncovered, at 350° for until eggs are completely set, 20-25 minutes.

2 muffin cups: 238cal., 15g fat (7g sat. fat), 452mg chol., 551mg sod., 3g carb. (2g sugars, 0 fiber), 22g pro.

HOW-TO

Test the Doneness of Hollandaise

Dip a spoon in the sauce and run your finger across the back. A fully cooked sauce will hold a firm line and not run down.

HAM & SWISS EGG CASSEROLE

Crunchy croissants top this simply satisfying dish. You can prep it the night before, pop it in the fridge and bake in the morning.
—Kathy Harding, Richmond, MO

PREP: 20 MIN. • **BAKE:** 35 MIN.
MAKES: 12 SERVINGS

- 16 large eggs
- 2 cups 2% milk
- ½ tsp. salt
- ¼ tsp. ground nutmeg
- 4 cups shredded Swiss cheese
- 8 oz. sliced deli ham, chopped
- 4 croissants, torn into 1½-in. pieces
- 1 Tbsp. minced chives

1. Preheat oven to 350°. Whisk together eggs, milk, salt and nutmeg. Sprinkle the cheese and ham into a greased 13x9-in. baking dish or pan; pour in egg mixture. Sprinkle croissant pieces over the top.
2. Bake, uncovered, until puffed and golden brown, 35-40 minutes. Sprinkle with chives. Let stand for 5-10 minutes before serving.

To make ahead: Refrigerate unbaked casserole, covered, for several hours or overnight. To use, preheat the oven to 350°. Remove the casserole from refrigerator while oven heats. Bake as directed.

1 piece: 354 cal., 23g fat (11g sat. fat), 306mg chol., 545mg sod., 12g carb. (5g sugars, 1g fiber), 24g pro.

SPINACH-EGG BREAKFAST PIZZAS

SPINACH-EGG BREAKFAST PIZZAS

Impress brunch guests with the elegance of these mini pizzas. I serve them with a bowl of fresh berries or grapes and cafe au lait.
—Lily Julow, Lawrenceville, GA

PREP: 20 MIN. • **BAKE:** 15 MIN.
MAKES: 4 PIZZAS

- Cornmeal
- 1 loaf (1 lb.) frozen pizza dough, thawed
- 1 Tbsp. plus additional extra virgin olive oil, divided
- 5 to 6 oz. fresh baby spinach
- ⅓ cup plus additional grated Parmesan cheese, divided
- 3 Tbsp. sour cream
- 1 small garlic clove, minced
- ¼ tsp. sea salt
- ⅛ tsp. plus additional coarsely ground pepper, divided
- 4 large eggs

1. Preheat the oven to 500°. Line two 15x10x1-in. baking pans with parchment; sprinkle lightly with cornmeal. Cut dough into 4 pieces; stretch and shape into 6- to 7-in. circles and place in pans.
2. Meanwhile, in a large skillet, heat 1 Tbsp. olive oil over medium-high heat. Add the spinach; cook and stir until just starting to wilt, 1-2 minutes. Combine the spinach with the next 5 ingredients; spread the spinach mixture over each pizza. Leave a slight border of raised dough along edge. Bake on lower oven rack about 5 minutes.
3. Remove from the oven; break an egg into the center of each pizza. Return to lower oven rack, baking until the egg whites are set but yolks are still runny, 6-10 minutes. Drizzle olive oil over the pizzas; top with additional Parmesan cheese and pepper. Serve immediately.

1 pizza: 433 cal., 14g fat (4g sat. fat), 199mg chol., 865mg sod., 55g carb. (3g sugars, 1g fiber), 16g pro.

VEGGIE-PACKED STRATA

Bursting with peppers, squash and more, this colorful casserole is a fabulous way to savor your fresh-picked garden produce.
—Jennifer Unsell, Vance, AL

PREP: 25 MIN.
BAKE: 1 HOUR 20 MIN. + STANDING
MAKES: 8 SERVINGS

- 2 medium sweet red peppers, julienned
- 1 medium sweet yellow pepper, julienned
- 1 large red onion, sliced
- 3 Tbsp. olive oil, divided
- 3 garlic cloves, minced
- 2 medium yellow summer squash, thinly sliced
- 2 medium zucchini, thinly sliced
- ½ pound fresh mushrooms, sliced
- 1 package (8 oz.) cream cheese, softened
- ¼ cup heavy whipping cream
- 2 tsp. salt
- 1 tsp. pepper
- 6 large eggs, room temperature
- 8 slices bread, cut into ½-in. cubes (about 6 cups), divided
- 2 cups shredded Swiss cheese

1. In a large skillet, saute the peppers and onion in 1 Tbsp. olive oil until tender. Add garlic; cook 1 minute longer. Drain; pat dry and set aside. In the same skillet, saute the yellow squash, zucchini and mushrooms in the remaining 2 Tbsp. oil until tender. Drain; pat dry and set aside.
2. Preheat oven to 325°. In a large bowl, beat cream cheese, heavy cream, salt and pepper until smooth. Beat in eggs. Stir in the vegetables, half of the bread cubes and Swiss cheese. Arrange the remaining bread cubes in a greased 10-in. springform pan. Place on baking sheet. Pour egg mixture into pan.
3. Bake, uncovered, for 80-95 minutes or until set and a thermometer reads 160°. Let stand for 10-15 minutes before serving. Run a knife around sides of pan to loosen; remove sides. Cut into wedges.
1 piece: 453 calories, 31g fat (15g saturated fat), 202mg cholesterol, 938mg sodium, 26g carbohydrate (8g sugars, 3g fiber), 19g protein.

SOUTHERN HASH BROWNS & HAM SHEET-PAN BAKE

I love the convenience of sheet-pan cooking. Here's a recipe that gives you a complete meal hot from the oven. Dig in!
—Colleen Delawder, Herndon, VA

PREP: 15 MIN. • **BAKE:** 35 MIN.
MAKES: 4 SERVINGS

- 1 pkg. (20 oz.) refrigerated shredded hash brown potatoes
- 3 Tbsp. olive oil
- ½ tsp. salt
- ½ tsp. pepper
- ¼ cup apple jelly
- ¼ cup apricot preserves
- 1 Tbsp. horseradish sauce
- 1 tsp. Dijon mustard
- ¼ tsp. garlic powder
- ¼ tsp. onion powder
- 2 cups cubed fully cooked ham
- 4 large eggs
- 2 green onions, finely chopped

1. Preheat oven to 400°. Place potatoes in a greased 15x10x1-in. baking pan. Drizzle with oil; sprinkle with salt and pepper. Toss to coat. Bake until edges are golden brown, 25-30 minutes.
2. In a small bowl, combine the jelly, preserves, horseradish sauce, Dijon, garlic powder and onion powder. Pour over potatoes; add ham. Toss to coat.
3. With the back of a spoon, make 4 wells in the potato mixture. Break an egg into each well. Bake until the egg whites are completely set and yolks begin to thicken but are not hard, 10-12 minutes. Sprinkle with green onions and additional pepper.
1 serving: 483 cal., 19g fat (4g sat. fat), 228mg chol., 1340mg sod., 55g carb. (23g sugars, 3g fiber), 24g pro.

VEGGIE-PACKED STRATA

Hot Breakfast Sides

Round out your a.m. spread with side dishes that make mornings memorable.

LATKES WITH LOX

Lox, a salty smoked salmon, is a year-round delicacy. This recipe, inspired by one from Jewish Journal, uses lox as a topping.
—*Taste of Home* Test Kitchen

PREP: 20 MIN. • **COOK:** 5 MIN./BATCH
MAKES: 3 DOZEN

- 2 cups finely chopped onion
- ¼ cup all-purpose flour
- 6 garlic cloves, minced
- 2 tsp. salt
- 1 tsp. coarsely ground pepper
- 4 large eggs, lightly beaten
- 4 lbs. russet potatoes, peeled and shredded
- ¾ cup canola oil
  TOPPINGS
- 4 oz. lox
  Optional: Sour cream and minced fresh chives

1. In a large bowl, combine the first 5 ingredients. Stir in eggs until blended. Add potatoes; toss to coat.
2. Heat 2 Tbsp. oil in a large nonstick skillet over medium heat. Drop batter by ¼ cupfuls into oil; press lightly to flatten. Fry in batches until golden brown on both sides, using remaining oil as needed. Drain on paper towels. Serve with lox; top with sour cream and chives if desired.
3 latkes with ⅓ oz. lox: 270 cal., 16g fat (2g sat. fat), 73mg chol., 610mg sod., 26g carb. (3g sugars, 2g fiber), 6g pro.

MAKE AHEAD
SLOW-COOKER GOETTA

My husband's German grandfather introduced me to goetta. I found a slow-cooker version, changed it a bit and ended up with the best goetta I've ever had.
—Sharon Geers, Wilmington, OH

PREP: 45 MIN. + CHILLING • **COOK:** 4 HOURS
MAKES: 2 LOAVES (16 SLICES EACH)

- 6 cups water
- 2½ cups steel-cut oats
- 6 bay leaves
- 3 Tbsp. beef bouillon granules
- ¾ tsp. salt
- 1 tsp. each garlic powder, rubbed sage and pepper
- ½ tsp. ground allspice
- ½ tsp. crushed red pepper flakes
- 2 lbs. bulk pork sausage
- 2 medium onions, chopped

1. In a 5-qt. slow cooker, combine water, oats and seasonings. Cook, covered, on high 2 hours. Remove bay leaves.
2. In a large skillet, cook the sausage and onions over medium heat until the meat is no longer pink, 8-10 minutes, breaking up the sausage into crumbles. Drain, reserving 2 Tbsp. drippings. Stir sausage mixture and reserved drippings into oats. Cook, covered, on low 2 hours.
3. Transfer mixture to 2 waxed paper-lined 9x5-in. loaf pans. Refrigerate, covered, overnight.
4. To serve, cut each loaf into 16 slices. In a large skillet, cook slices in batches over medium heat until lightly browned and heated through, 3-4 minutes on each side.
Freeze option: After shaping the goetta in loaf pans, cool and freeze, covered, until firm. Transfer the goetta to freezer containers or wrap securely in foil; return to freezer. Partially thaw in refrigerator overnight; slice and cook as directed.
1 slice: 121 cal., 7g fat (2g sat. fat), 15mg chol., 450mg sod., 10g carb. (1g sugars, 1g fiber), 5g pro.

SLOW-COOKER
GOETTA

MUSHROOM-GRUYERE SCALLOPED POTATOES

SALSA CORN CAKES

Spice up any morning with Tex-Mex cakes that have a subtle salsa flavor. For lunch or dinner, serve them alongside nachos or tacos. I like to replace the canned corn with fresh when it's in season.

—Lisa Boettcher, Rosebush, MI

TAKES: 20 MIN. • **MAKES:** 8 SERVINGS

- 6 oz. cream cheese, softened
- ¼ cup butter, melted
- 6 large eggs, room temperature
- 1 cup 2% milk
- 1½ cups all-purpose flour
- ½ cup cornmeal
- 1 tsp. baking powder
- 1 tsp. salt
- 1 can (15¼ oz.) whole kernel corn, drained
- ½ cup salsa, drained
- ¼ cup minced green onions
  Sour cream and additional salsa

1. In a large bowl, beat cream cheese and butter until smooth; add the eggs and mix well. Beat in milk until smooth. Combine flour, cornmeal, baking powder and salt; stir into cream cheese mixture just until moistened. Fold in corn, salsa and onions.
2. Pour batter by ¼ cupfuls into a large greased cast-iron skillet or hot griddle. Turn when bubbles form on top; cook until the second side is golden brown. Serve with sour cream and salsa.
1 serving: 324 cal., 15g fat (8g sat. fat), 191mg chol., 715mg sod., 34g carb. (5g sugars, 3g fiber), 11g pro.

MUSHROOM-GRUYERE SCALLOPED POTATOES

When I began cooking, the only mushrooms I used were the button variety. Now I enjoy experimenting with different types, including the shiitakes and portobellos in this potato favorite. It's great not only for brunch, but also with a steak or ham entree—and even as a meatless main dish with a green salad.

—Nadine Mesch, Mount Healthy, OH

PREP: 30 MIN. • **BAKE:** 1 HOUR + STANDING
MAKES: 10 SERVINGS

- 6 Tbsp. butter, divided
- ½ lb. each sliced fresh shiitake, baby portobello and button mushrooms
- 1 Tbsp. sherry, optional
- 5 Tbsp. all-purpose flour
- 3 cups half-and-half cream
- 3 Tbsp. minced fresh rosemary
- 1½ tsp. salt
- 1 tsp. pepper
- 2 cups shredded Gruyere cheese
- 2 lbs. red potatoes, thinly sliced
- ½ tsp. paprika

1. Preheat oven to 350°. In a large skillet, heat 1 Tbsp. butter over medium-high heat. Add mushrooms; cook and stir until tender. If desired, stir in sherry and cook until evaporated, 1-2 minutes longer. Remove from pan.
2. In the same pan, melt the remaining butter over medium heat. Stir in flour until smooth; gradually whisk in cream. Bring to a boil, stirring constantly; cook and stir until thickened, about 2 minutes. Reduce the heat to medium-low. Stir in minced rosemary, salt and pepper. Gradually add the cheese, stirring until melted. Remove from heat.
3. Arrange the potatoes in an even layer in a greased 13x9-in. baking dish. Top with the mushrooms and sauce mixture; sprinkle with paprika.
4. Bake, covered, 40 minutes. Bake, uncovered, until golden brown and bubbly, 20-25 minutes longer. Let stand 15 minutes before serving.
¾ cup: 442 cal., 29g fat (18g sat. fat), 104mg chol., 599mg sod., 23g carb. (4g sugars, 3g fiber), 20g pro.

MUFFIN-TIN TAMALE CAKES

Savor all the tamale flavor you love without the fuss! These little corn cakes are so good in the morning or as a snack any time of day. Pair them with fresh fruit skewers.
—Suzanne Clark, Phoenix, AZ

PREP: 25 MIN. • **BAKE:** 20 MIN.
MAKES: 2 DOZEN

- 2 pkg. (8½ oz. each) cornbread/muffin mix
- 1 can (14¾ oz.) cream-style corn
- 2 large eggs, room temperature, lightly beaten
- 1½ cups shredded reduced-fat Mexican cheese blend, divided
- 1½ cups chopped cooked chicken breast
- ¾ cup red enchilada sauce

1. Preheat oven to 400°. In a large bowl, combine the muffin mix, corn and eggs; stir just until moistened. Stir in 1 cup cheese. In another bowl, toss chicken with enchilada sauce.
2. Fill each of 24 foil-lined muffin cups with 2 Tbsp. batter. Place 1 Tbsp. chicken mixture into center of each; cover with about 1 Tbsp. of batter.
3. Bake until muffins are golden brown, 13-15 minutes. Sprinkle the tops with remaining cheese. Bake until the cheese is melted, 3-5 minutes longer. Cool for 5 minutes before removing from the pan to wire racks. Serve warm. Refrigerate any leftovers.
1 muffin: 137 cal., 5g fat (2g sat. fat), 28mg chol., 313mg sod., 18g carb. (5g sugars, 2g fiber), 7g pro.
Diabetic exchanges: 1 starch, 1 lean meat.

CHEESY SAUSAGE POTATOES

A crowd-pleasing breakfast can be as simple as these tender potato slices loaded with sausage, onions and cheese.
—Linda Hill, Marseilles, IL

TAKES: 25 MIN. • **MAKES:** 10 SERVINGS

- 3 lbs. potatoes, peeled and cut into ¼-in. slices
- 1 lb. bulk pork sausage
- 1 medium onion, chopped
- ¼ cup butter, melted
- 2 cups shredded cheddar cheese

1. Place potatoes in a large saucepan and cover with water. Bring to a boil. Reduce heat; simmer, uncovered, until tender, 8-10 minutes.
2. Meanwhile, crumble the sausage into a large skillet; add the onion. Cook over medium heat until the meat is no longer pink; drain if necessary.
3. Drain the potatoes; arrange in an ungreased 13x9-in. baking dish. Drizzle with butter. Add sausage mixture and stir gently. Sprinkle with cheese.
4. Bake, uncovered, at 350° until cheese is melted, 5-7 minutes.
¾ cup: 252 cal., 13g fat (8g sat. fat), 37mg chol., 220mg sod., 26g carb. (2g sugars, 3g fiber), 9g pro.

HOW-TO

Grate Cheese with Less Mess

A spritz of cooking spray will keep cheese from sticking to the grater and make cleanup easier.

CHEESY SAUSAGE POTATOES

ORANGE-GLAZED BACON
Think bacon can't get any tastier? Here's an amazing citrus version that just might change your mind!
—*Taste of Home* Test Kitchen

PREP: 20 MIN. • **BAKE:** 25 MIN.
MAKES: 8 SERVINGS

- ¾ cup orange juice
- ¼ cup honey
- 1 Tbsp. Dijon mustard
- ¼ tsp. ground ginger
- ⅛ tsp. pepper
- 1 lb. bacon strips

1. In a small saucepan, combine the first 5 ingredients. Bring to a boil; cook until liquid is reduced to ⅓ cup.
2. Place bacon on a rack in an ungreased 15x10x1-in. baking pan. Bake at 350° for 10 minutes; drain.
3. Drizzle half of the glaze over bacon. Bake for 10 minutes. Turn bacon and drizzle with the remaining glaze. Bake 5-10 minutes longer or until golden brown. Place bacon on waxed paper until set. Serve warm.

3 glazed bacon strips: 146 cal., 8g fat (3g sat. fat), 21mg chol., 407mg sod., 12g carb. (11g sugars, 0 fiber), 7g pro.

LEMON MINT BEANS
Warm-weather meals call for refreshing food. Brightened with lemon and mint, these easy green beans make a delightful addition to a summer brunch.
—Dorothy Pritchett, Wills Point, TX

TAKES: 10 MIN. • **MAKES:** 4 SERVINGS

- 1 lb. fresh or frozen cut green beans or wax beans
- 1 Tbsp. lemon juice
- 1 Tbsp. snipped fresh mint
- ¼ tsp. grated lemon zest
- ½ tsp. salt

In a saucepan, cook the beans in a small amount of water until tender; drain. Add the remaining ingredients; toss to coat.

1 cup: 39 cal., 0 fat (0 sat. fat), 0 chol., 297mg sod., 9g carb. (0 sugars, 3g fiber), 2g pro.
Diabetic exchanges: 2 vegetable.

BAVARIAN HARVEST APPLE HASH

Looking for something to warm up a chilly fall or winter morning? This comforting hash featuring apple chicken sausage and chopped apple is hard to beat. The recipe reflects my family's German roots.

—Crystal Schlueter, Northglenn, CO

TAKES: 30 MIN. • **MAKES:** 4 SERVINGS

- 2 Tbsp. canola oil
- ½ cup chopped onion
- 4 fully cooked apple chicken sausages or flavor of your choice, sliced
- 1½ cups thinly sliced Brussels sprouts
- 1 large tart apple, peeled and chopped
- 1 tsp. caraway seeds
- ¼ tsp. salt
- ⅛ tsp. pepper
- 2 Tbsp. finely chopped walnuts
- 1 Tbsp. brown sugar
- 1 Tbsp. whole grain mustard
- 1 Tbsp. cider vinegar

1. In a large skillet, heat the oil over medium-high heat; saute onion until tender, 1-2 minutes. Add sausages, Brussels sprouts, apple and seasonings; saute until lightly browned, 6-8 minutes.
2. Stir in walnuts, brown sugar, mustard and vinegar; cook and stir 2 minutes.

1 cup: 310 cal., 17g fat (3g sat. fat), 60mg chol., 715mg sod., 25g carb. (19g sugars, 3g fiber), 16g pro.

PEPPER JACK HASH BROWN CASSEROLE

PEPPER JACK HASH BROWN CASSEROLE

When I needed a potato dish quickly but was out of potatoes, I used a bag of frozen hash browns instead. Success!

—Cyndy Gerken, Naples, FL

PREP: 25 MIN. • **BAKE:** 30 MIN.
MAKES: 12 SERVINGS

- 1 pkg. (30 oz.) frozen shredded hash brown potatoes, thawed
- 1 can (10½ oz.) condensed cream of chicken soup, undiluted
- 2 cups shredded pepper jack cheese
- 1½ cups heavy whipping cream
- ½ cup butter, melted
- ½ cup sour cream
- ¼ cup shredded Parmesan cheese
- ½ tsp. salt
- ½ tsp. onion powder
- ¼ tsp. garlic powder
- ¼ tsp. pepper

TOPPING
- 1 cup crushed potato chips
- 5 bacon strips, cooked and crumbled
- ¾ cup shredded Parmesan cheese
- 1 tsp. paprika

1. Preheat oven to 350°. In a large bowl, combine first 11 ingredients. Transfer to a greased 13x9-in. baking dish. For topping, combine potato chips, bacon and Parmesan; sprinkle over casserole. Top with paprika.
2. Bake, uncovered, until the edges are bubbly and the topping is golden brown, 25-30 minutes.

⅔ cup: 416 cal., 33g fat (19g sat. fat), 87mg chol., 682mg sod., 20g carb. (2g sugars, 2g fiber), 12g pro.

BRIGHT IDEA

If you're making this dish for kiddos or an adult who doesn't like spicy food, use Monterey Jack cheese instead of pepper jack.

BOHEMIAN COLLARDS

Unconventional ingredients make these collard greens delightfully different.
—Ally Phillips, Murrells Inlet, SC

PREP: 20 MIN. • **COOK:** 35 MIN.
MAKES: 8 SERVINGS

- 1 large bunch collard greens (about 2 lbs.)
- 6 bacon strips, chopped
- 1 Tbsp. olive oil
- ½ cup chicken broth
- 1½ cups fresh or frozen corn (about 7½ oz.)
- 1 cup chopped sweet red pepper
- ½ tsp. salt
- ¼ tsp. crushed red pepper flakes
- ¼ tsp. pepper

1. Trim thick stems from collard greens; coarsely chop leaves. In a Dutch oven, cook the bacon over medium heat until crisp, stirring occasionally. Remove with a slotted spoon; drain on paper towels. Cook and stir collard greens in bacon drippings and olive oil just until coated. Add broth; bring to a boil. Reduce heat; simmer, covered, until greens are very tender, 25-30 minutes.
2. Add corn, red pepper, salt, pepper flakes and pepper. Cook and stir until heated through. Sprinkle with bacon.
½ cup: 168 cal., 11g fat (3g sat. fat), 14mg chol., 369mg sod., 13g carb. (2g sugars, 5g fiber), 7g pro.
Diabetic exchanges: 2 fat, 1 starch.

MAKE AHEAD
BACON CHEESE MUFFINS

For brunch or anytime, you can't go wrong with savory muffins of bacon, cheese and more. Store an extra batch in the freezer, and then reheat as many as you need on busy mornings before school or work.
—Kendra Schertz, Nappanee, IN

PREP: 15 MIN. • **BAKE:** 20 MIN.
MAKES: 8 SERVINGS

- 6 oz. cream cheese, softened
- 5 tsp. 2% milk
- 2 large eggs, room temperature
- ½ cup shredded Colby cheese
- 2 Tbsp. chopped green pepper
- 1 Tbsp. finely chopped onion
- 1 tube (8 oz.) refrigerated crescent rolls
- 5 bacon strips, cooked and crumbled Sliced green onions, optional

1. In a small bowl, beat cream cheese and milk until smooth. Add eggs, cheese, green pepper and onion.
2. Separate the crescent roll dough into 8 triangles; press onto the bottom and up the sides of greased muffin cups. Sprinkle half of the bacon into the cups. Pour egg mixture over bacon; top with remaining bacon.
3. Bake at 375° for 18-22 minutes or until a knife inserted in the center comes out clean. Serve warm. If desired, top with sliced green onion.
Freeze option: Freeze the cooled muffins in a freezer container. To use, heat on a baking sheet in a preheated 375° oven until heated through.
1 muffin: 258 cal., 19g fat (9g sat. fat), 87mg chol., 409mg sod., 12g carb. (3g sugars, 0 fiber), 8g pro.

BOHEMIAN COLLARDS

SWEET POTATO PANCAKES WITH CINNAMON CREAM

Dolloped with a cinnamon cream topping, these cakes are a wonderful way to savor the flavors and aromas of fall.

—Tammy Rex, New Tripoli, PA

PREP: 25 MIN. • **COOK:** 5 MIN./BATCH
MAKES: 24 PANCAKES (1½ CUPS TOPPING)

- 1 pkg. (8 oz.) cream cheese, softened
- ¼ cup packed brown sugar
- ½ tsp. ground cinnamon
- ½ cup sour cream

PANCAKES

- 6 large eggs, room temperature
- ¾ cup all-purpose flour
- ½ tsp. ground nutmeg
- ½ tsp. salt
- ¼ tsp. pepper
- 6 cups shredded peeled sweet potatoes (about 3 large)
- 3 cups shredded peeled apples (about 3 large)
- ⅓ cup grated onion
- ½ cup canola oil

1. In a small bowl, beat the cream cheese, brown sugar and cinnamon until blended; beat in the sour cream. Set the mixture aside.

2. In a large bowl, whisk the eggs, flour, nutmeg, salt and pepper. Add the sweet potatoes, apples and onion; toss to coat.

3. In a large nonstick skillet, heat 2 Tbsp. canola oil over medium heat. Working in batches, drop sweet potato mixture by ⅓ cupfuls into the oil; press slightly to flatten. Fry 2-3 minutes on each side or until golden brown, using remaining oil as needed. Drain on paper towels. Serve with cinnamon topping.

2 pancakes with 2 Tbsp. topping: 325 cal., 21g fat (7g sat. fat), 114mg chol., 203mg sod., 30g carb. (15g sugars, 3g fiber), 6g pro.

SWEET POTATO PANCAKES WITH CINNAMON CREAM

PUMPKIN & CHICKEN
SAUSAGE HASH

PUMPKIN & CHICKEN SAUSAGE HASH

Whether you have it as a side or a main dish, this hearty hash offers plenty of home-style goodness. I like serving poached or fried eggs on top for a complete meal.
—Valerie Donn, Williamsburg, MI

PREP: 15 MIN. • **COOK:** 25 MIN.
MAKES: 4 SERVINGS

- 2 Tbsp. olive oil
- 2 cups cubed fresh pumpkin or butternut squash
- ¼ tsp. salt
- ¼ tsp. pepper
- ½ cup chopped onion
- 1 pkg. (12 oz.) fully cooked apple chicken sausage links or flavor of your choice, cut into ½-in. slices
- 1 cup sliced fresh mushrooms
- ½ cup chopped sweet red pepper
- ½ cup chopped green pepper
- 1 tsp. garlic powder
- ¼ cup minced fresh parsley

In a large skillet, heat the olive oil over medium heat. Add pumpkin; sprinkle with salt and pepper. Cook and stir until crisp-tender, 8-10 minutes. Add onion; cook 3 minutes longer. Add chicken sausage, mushrooms, red and green pepper and garlic powder. Cook and stir 10-12 minutes or until the pumpkin is tender. Top with fresh minced parsley before serving.
1 serving: 260 cal., 14g fat (3g sat. fat), 60mg chol., 634mg sod., 19g carb. (13g sugars, 2g fiber), 16g pro.
Diabetic exchanges: 2 lean meat, 1½ fat, 1 starch.

BAKED FRUIT COMPOTE

A splash of Madeira wine turns a compote of canned fruit into something extra special. It's sure to brighten up your winter brunch.
—Myrt Pfannkuche, Pell City, AL

TAKES: 30 MIN. • **MAKES:** 11 SERVINGS

- 1 can (29 oz.) sliced peaches, drained
- 1 can (20 oz.) pineapple chunks, drained
- 2 cans (8 oz. each) grapefruit sections, drained
- 1 can (15¼ oz.) sliced pears, drained
- 1 can (11 oz.) mandarin oranges, drained
- 1 cup pitted dried plums
- ½ cup butter, cubed
- ½ cup packed brown sugar
- ¼ cup Madeira wine, optional
  Fresh mint leaves, optional

1. Preheat the oven to 350°. In a 13x9-in. baking dish, combine first 6 ingredients.
2. In a small saucepan, combine butter and brown sugar. Bring to a boil over medium heat; cook and stir until sugar is dissolved, 2-3 minutes. Remove from heat; stir in Madeira wine if desired. Pour over fruit and toss to coat.
3. Bake, uncovered, until heated through, 20-25 minutes. Garnish with mint leaves if desired.
¾ cup: 257 cal., 8g fat (5g sat. fat), 22mg chol., 75mg sod., 46g carb. (39g sugars, 2g fiber), 1g pro.

Brunch-Worthy Sandwiches

Meet the delicious handhelds that
make for glorious mornings.

THE BEST EVER GRILLED CHEESE SANDWICH

Here's the one you've been waiting for! Spreading a mix of mayo and butter on the bread creates a delightfully crispy crust.
—Josh Rink, Milwaukee, WI

TAKES: 25 MIN. • **MAKES:** 4 SERVINGS

- 6 Tbsp. butter, softened, divided
- 8 slices sourdough bread
- 3 Tbsp. mayonnaise
- 3 Tbsp. finely shredded Manchego or Parmesan cheese
- ⅛ tsp. onion powder
- ½ cup shredded sharp white cheddar cheese
- ½ cup shredded Monterey Jack cheese
- ½ cup shredded Gruyere cheese
- 4 oz. Brie cheese, rind removed, sliced

1. Spread 3 Tbsp. butter on 1 side of bread slices. Toast the bread, butter side down, in a large skillet or electric griddle over medium-low heat until golden brown, 2-3 minutes; remove. In a small bowl, mix together the mayonnaise, Manchego cheese, onion powder and remaining 3 Tbsp. butter. In another bowl, combine the cheddar, Monterey Jack and Gruyere.
2. To assemble sandwiches, top toasted side of 4 bread slices with sliced Brie. Sprinkle cheddar mixture evenly over Brie. Top with remaining bread slices, toasted side facing inward. Spread the mayonnaise mixture on outsides of each sandwich. Place in same skillet and cook until bread is golden brown and cheese is melted, 5-6 minutes on each side. Serve immediately.
1 sandwich: 659 cal., 49g fat (27g sat. fat), 122mg chol., 1017mg sod., 30g carb. (3g sugars, 1g fiber), 24g pro.

STRAWBERRY MONTE CRISTOS

A gooey Monte Cristo never fails to please. Sweetened with a side of berry preserves, my version comes together quickly with deli meats and bottled salad dressing.
—Debbie Brunssen, Randolph, NE

TAKES: 25 MIN. • **MAKES:** 4 SERVINGS

- ¼ cup mayonnaise
- 2 tsp. Thousand Island salad dressing
- 1 tsp. Dijon mustard
- 8 slices white bread
- ¼ lb. thinly sliced deli turkey
- ¼ lb. thinly sliced deli ham
- 4 slices Swiss cheese
- 2 large eggs, beaten
- 1 cup half-and-half cream
- ¼ tsp. ground mustard
- 2 Tbsp. butter
- ¼ cup strawberry preserves

1. In a small bowl, combine mayonnaise, salad dressing and mustard; spread over 1 side of each slice of bread. On 4 slices, layer turkey, ham and Swiss cheese; top with remaining bread. In a shallow bowl, combine eggs, cream and ground mustard. Dip sandwiches in egg mixture.
2. On a griddle or in a large skillet, melt the butter. Toast the sandwiches over medium heat for 2-3 minutes on each side or until the bread is golden brown. Serve sandwiches with preserves.
1 sandwich: 630 cal., 36g fat (15g sat. fat), 185mg chol., 1208mg sod., 46g carb. (18g sugars, 2g fiber),

THE BEST EVER GRILLED CHEESE SANDWICH

CROQUE-MADAME

ATHENIAN CHICKEN GRILLED CHEESE SANDWICHES

Mozzarella, feta and Parmesan make a delicious trio in this upscale sandwich featuring chicken and fresh herbs.
—Michael Cohen, Los Angeles, CA

TAKES: 30 MIN. • **MAKES:** 4 SERVINGS

- 1 lb. boneless skinless chicken breasts, cubed
- ¼ tsp. kosher salt
- ¼ tsp. pepper
- 3 garlic cloves, minced
- 1 Tbsp. plus ¼ cup olive oil, divided
- 6 oz. fresh mozzarella cheese, shredded
- ½ cup crumbled feta cheese
- ½ cup grated Parmesan cheese
- ½ cup fresh mint leaves, chopped
- 2 Tbsp. minced fresh oregano
- 2 Tbsp. capers, drained
- 8 slices olive or Italian bread (½ in. thick)

1. Sprinkle chicken with salt and pepper. In a large skillet, cook chicken and garlic in 1 Tbsp. olive oil over medium heat until meat is no longer pink. Set aside and keep warm.
2. In a small bowl, combine cheeses, mint, oregano and capers. Distribute half the cheese mixture evenly among 4 bread slices. Layer with the chicken and remaining cheese mixture. Top with the remaining bread. Brush the outsides of sandwiches with remaining oil.
3. On a griddle, toast the sandwiches for 2-3 minutes on each side or until cheese is melted.
1 sandwich: 605 cal., 36g fat (13g sat. fat), 112mg chol., 918mg sod., 27g carb. (1g sugars, 3g fiber), 41g pro.

CROQUE-MADAME

My son and I prefer to top this grilled ham and cheese with a fried egg, but you can make yours without it (and that creates a croque-monsieur).
—Carolyn Turner, Reno, NV

TAKES: 30 MIN. • **MAKES:** 8 SERVINGS

- 1 lb. thinly sliced Gruyere cheese, divided
- 16 slices sourdough bread
- 1½ lbs. thinly sliced deli ham
- ½ cup butter, softened
- 4 to 6 Tbsp. mayonnaise

EGGS
- 2 Tbsp. butter
- 8 large eggs
- ½ tsp. salt
- ½ tsp. pepper

1. Preheat oven to 400°. Place half the cheese on 8 bread slices; top with the deli ham and remaining bread. Spread the outsides of the sandwiches with softened butter.
2. On a griddle, toast sandwiches over medium heat 2-3 minutes on each side or until golden brown. Spread the tops with mayonnaise; top with the remaining cheese. Transfer to an ungreased baking sheet; bake 4-5 minutes or until cheese is melted.
3. Meanwhile, for the eggs, heat 1 Tbsp. butter on a griddle over medium-high heat. Break 4 eggs, 1 at a time, onto the griddle. Reduce heat to low. Cook to the desired doneness, turning after whites are set if desired. Sprinkle with salt and pepper. Place eggs over sandwiches. Repeat with remaining ingredients.
1 sandwich: 758 cal., 47g fat (24g sat. fat), 344mg chol., 1691mg sod., 40g carb. (2g sugars, 2g fiber), 46g pro.

CHICKEN FLORENTINE PANINI

ENGLISH MUFFIN EGG SANDWICHES

Add peppers, mushrooms, onions and seasonings to scrambled eggs, then pile them onto a toasted English muffin slathered with cream cheese. What a way to start the day! If you prefer less spice, simply leave out the red pepper flakes.
—Amy Lloyd, Madison, WI

TAKES: 25 MIN. • **MAKES:** 8 SERVINGS

- 4 tsp. canola oil, divided
- ½ lb. sliced fresh mushrooms
- 1 small sweet red pepper, chopped
- 1 small sweet onion, chopped
- ½ tsp. garlic salt
- ¼ tsp. pepper
- ¼ tsp. crushed red pepper flakes, optional
- 7 large eggs, lightly beaten
- 8 whole wheat English muffins, split and toasted
- 4 oz. reduced-fat cream cheese

1. In a large skillet, heat 2 tsp. oil over medium heat. Add the mushrooms, red pepper, onion, garlic salt, pepper and red pepper flakes; cook and stir 5-7 minutes or until mushrooms are tender. Remove from pan.
2. Wipe the skillet clean. Heat remaining 2 tsp. oil over medium heat. Add eggs; cook and stir just until the eggs are thickened and no liquid egg remains. Add vegetable mixture; heat through, stirring gently.
3. Spread muffin bottoms with cream cheese; top with egg mixture. Replace the tops.
1 sandwich: 244 cal., 9g fat (4g sat. fat), 173mg chol., 425mg sod., 30g carb. (7g sugars, 5g fiber), 14g pro.
Diabetic exchanges: 2 starch, 1 medium-fat meat, ½ fat.

CHICKEN FLORENTINE PANINI

This cheesy grilled sandwich is so good, you'll want one for brunch and dinner, too.
—Lee Bremson, Kansas City, MO

TAKES: 25 MIN. • **MAKES:** 4 SERVINGS

- 1 pkg. (5 oz.) fresh baby spinach
- 2 tsp. olive oil
- ¼ cup butter, softened
- 8 slices sourdough bread
- ¼ cup creamy Italian salad dressing
- 8 slices provolone cheese
- ½ lb. shaved deli chicken
- 2 slices red onion, separated into rings

1. In a large cast-iron or other heavy skillet, saute the spinach in oil until wilted, about 2 minutes. Drain; wipe the skillet clean.
2. Spread 4 bread slices with the salad dressing. Layer with a provolone cheese slice, deli chicken, spinach, red onion and another cheese slice. Top with remaining bread. Butter outsides of sandwiches.
3. Cook in same skillet or a panini maker until bread is golden brown and cheese is melted.
1 sandwich: 582 cal., 26g fat (10g sat. fat), 62mg chol., 1688mg sod., 63g carb. (4g sugars, 5g fiber), 23g pro.

ENGLISH MUFFIN
EGG SANDWICHES

HUMMUS & VEGGIE WRAP-UP

At a diner I stopped at once during a long walk, I discovered a wrap stuffed with different vegetables. I liked it so much, I experimented a bit at home and came up with my own version. Now I eat it for lunch regularly, and everyone who tries it requests the recipe.
—Michael Steffens, Indianapolis, IN

TAKES: 15 MIN. • **MAKES:** 1 SERVING

- 2 Tbsp. hummus
- 1 whole wheat tortilla (8 in.)
- ¼ cup torn mixed salad greens
- 2 Tbsp. finely chopped sweet onion
- 2 Tbsp. thinly sliced cucumber
- 2 Tbsp. alfalfa sprouts
- 2 Tbsp. shredded carrot
- 1 Tbsp. balsamic vinaigrette

Spread hummus over tortilla. Layer with salad greens, onion, cucumber, sprouts and carrot. Drizzle with vinaigrette. Roll up tightly.

1 wrap: 235 cal., 8g fat (1g sat. fat), 0 chol., 415mg sod., 32g carb. (4g sugars, 5g fiber), 7g pro.
Diabetic exchanges: 2 starch, 1 fat.

READER REVIEW

"I love how this wrap is different from the everyday. Drizzled with balsamic vinaigrette and spread with hummus, the veggie-stuffed tortilla tastes gourmet but is so quick and casual for a brunch, lunch or snack. I prepared these for guests, and everyone raved about them. It is absolutely a little gem of a recipe."
— MARINA, TASTEOFHOME.COM

BREAKFAST BURGER

BREAKFAST BURGER

My husband is a big fan of eggs and bacon. For an over-the-top morning treat, I loaded his breakfast favorites onto a grilled burger.
—Tina Janssen, Walworth, WI

PREP: 25 MIN. • **GRILL:** 30 MIN.
MAKES: 4 SERVINGS

- 1 lb. ground beef
- 1 Tbsp. Worcestershire sauce
- 1 tsp. Montreal steak seasoning
- ½ tsp. salt, divided
- ½ tsp. pepper, divided
- 3 Tbsp. butter, softened and divided
- 8 slices Texas toast
- 2 Tbsp. canola oil
- 2½ cups frozen shredded hash brown potatoes, thawed
- 4 large eggs
- ¼ cup seedless blackberry spreadable fruit
- 4 slices American cheese
- 8 cooked bacon strips

1. Combine beef, Worcestershire, steak seasoning, ¼ tsp. salt and ¼ tsp. pepper; mix lightly but thoroughly. Shape into four ½-in.-thick patties. Grill burgers, covered, on a greased grill rack over medium heat until a thermometer reads 160°, 4-5 minutes on each side.

2. Meanwhile, spread 2 Tbsp. butter over 1 side of toast slices; grill with burgers until golden brown. Remove burgers and toast from heat; keep warm.
3. Increase heat to high. In a large skillet on grill rack, heat oil. Drop hash browns by ½ cupfuls into the oil; press to flatten. Sprinkle with remaining salt and pepper. Fry, covered, until golden brown and crisp, 12-15 minutes on each side, adding oil as needed. Remove and keep warm.
4. Reduce heat to medium. In the same skillet, heat remaining butter. Add eggs; fry over easy.
5. To assemble, spread the blackberry spread over 4 slices of toast. Layer each slice with 1 hash brown patty, 1 burger, 1 fried egg, 1 cheese slice and 2 bacon strips. Top with remaining toast slices.

1 burger: 859 cal., 49g fat (19g sat. fat), 307mg chol., 1703mg sod., 55g carb. (13g sugars, 2g fiber), 45g pro.

SALMON CROQUETTE BREAKFAST SANDWICH

I'm obsessed with smoked salmon on bagels! I could eat it every day for breakfast. But smoked salmon can get pricey, so I use an economical alternative that gives me the flavor I crave.
—Jessi Hampton, Richmond Hill, GA

PREP: 25 MIN. • **COOK:** 10 MIN.
MAKES: 2 SERVINGS

- 1 large egg, lightly beaten
- ¼ cup dry bread crumbs
- 1 tsp. garlic powder
- 1 tsp. smoked paprika
- 1 pouch (6 oz.) boneless skinless pink salmon
- 1 Tbsp. olive oil
- 2 everything bagels, split and toasted
- 4 Tbsp. cream cheese, softened
- 1 Tbsp. capers, drained
- 1 medium tomato, sliced
- ½ medium red onion, thinly sliced into rings
- Snipped fresh dill, optional

1. In a small bowl, combine the egg, bread crumbs, garlic powder and smoked paprika. Add salmon and mix lightly but thoroughly. Shape into 2 patties.
2. In a large skillet, cook the patties in oil over medium heat until browned, 5-6 minutes on each side. Spread the bagels with cream cheese; top with capers. Serve patties on bagels with tomato, onion and, if desired, dill.

1 sandwich: 656 cal., 25g fat (10g sat. fat), 152mg chol., 1205mg sod., 75g carb. (14g sugars, 4g fiber), 34g pro.

SALMON CROQUETTE BREAKFAST SANDWICH

TOAD IN THE HOLE BACON SANDWICH

Switch up the cheese—pepper jack adds a nice kick—or use sliced kielbasa, ham or sausage instead of bacon in this versatile grilled cheese sandwich.
—Kallee Krong-McCreery, Escondido, CA

TAKES: 15 MIN. • **MAKES:** 1 SERVING

- 2 slices sourdough bread
- 1 Tbsp. mayonnaise
- 1 large egg
- 1 slice cheddar cheese
- 2 cooked bacon strips

1. Using a biscuit cutter or round cookie cutter, cut out center of 1 slice of bread (discard center or save for another use). Spread mayonnaise on 1 side of the bread slices. In a large skillet coated with cooking spray, lightly toast the cutout slice, mayonnaise side down, over medium-low heat. Flip slice; crack an egg into center. Add the remaining bread slice, mayonnaise side down, to skillet; layer with cheese and bacon.
2. Cook, covered, until the egg white is set, yolk is soft-set and cheese begins to melt. If needed, flip slice with the egg to finish cooking. To assemble sandwich, use solid bread slice as the bottom and cutout slice as the top.

1 sandwich: 610 cal., 34g fat (11g sat. fat), 240mg chol., 1220mg sod., 46g carb. (4g sugars, 2g fiber), 30g pro.

Midday Mains

Find the ideal dish for that magical time when morning, noon and beyond blend into one incredible meal.

CAPRESE CHICKEN WITH BACON

Smoky bacon, fresh basil, ripe tomatoes and gooey mozzarella top these Italian chicken breasts. The aroma that fills the kitchen as they bake is irresistible!
—Tammy Hayden, Quincy, MI

PREP: 20 MIN. • **BAKE:** 20 MIN.
MAKES: 4 SERVINGS

- 8 bacon strips
- 4 boneless skinless chicken breast halves (6 oz. each)
- 1 Tbsp. olive oil
- ½ tsp. salt
- ¼ tsp. pepper
- 2 plum tomatoes, sliced
- 6 fresh basil leaves, thinly sliced
- 4 slices part-skim mozzarella cheese

1. Place the bacon in an ungreased 15x10x1-in. baking pan. Bake at 400° until partially cooked but not crisp, 8-10 minutes. Remove to paper towels to drain.
2. Place the chicken in an ungreased 13x9-in. baking pan; brush with olive oil and sprinkle with salt and pepper. Top with the plum tomatoes and basil. Wrap each in 2 bacon strips, arranging bacon in a crisscross.
3. Bake, uncovered, at 400° until a thermometer inserted in the chicken reads 165°, 15-20 minutes. Top with mozzarella; bake until melted, about 1 minute longer.
1 chicken breast half: 373 cal., 18g fat (7g sat. fat), 123mg chol., 821mg sod., 3g carb. (1g sugars, 0 fiber), 47g pro.

SPICY BREAKFAST LASAGNA

It's fun to cook something new for family members and friends—especially when it's a hit! When I surprised our breakfast club at work with a zippy lasagna, my co-workers said it woke up their taste buds.
—Guthrie Torp Jr., Highland Ranch, CO

PREP: 20 MIN. + CHILLING
BAKE: 35 MIN. • **MAKES:** 16 SERVINGS

- 3 cups 4% cottage cheese
- ½ cup minced chives
- ¼ cup sliced green onions
- 18 large eggs
- ⅓ cup 2% milk
- ½ tsp. salt
- ¼ tsp. pepper
- 1 Tbsp. butter
- 8 lasagna noodles, cooked and drained
- 4 cups frozen shredded hash browns, thawed
- 1 lb. bulk pork sausage, cooked and crumbled
- 8 oz. sliced Monterey Jack cheese with jalapeno peppers
- 8 oz. sliced Muenster cheese

1. Combine the cottage cheese, chives and onions; set aside. In another bowl, whisk eggs, milk, salt and pepper until blended. In a large skillet, heat butter over medium heat. Pour in egg mixture; cook and stir until the eggs are thickened and no liquid egg remains. Remove from heat; set aside.
2. Place 4 lasagna noodles in a greased 13x9-in. baking dish. Layer with 2 cups hash browns, scrambled eggs, sausage and half the cottage cheese mixture. Cover with Monterey Jack cheese. Top with remaining noodles, hash browns and cottage cheese mixture. Cover with Muenster cheese. Refrigerate, covered, for 8 hours or overnight.
3. Remove dish from the refrigerator 30 minutes before baking. Preheat oven to 350°. Bake, uncovered, until a knife inserted in the center comes out clean, 35-40 minutes. Let stand 5 minutes before cutting.
1 piece: 366 cal., 23g fat (11g sat. fat), 256mg chol., 640mg sod., 16g carb. (3g sugars, 1g fiber), 23g pro.

SPICY BREAKFAST LASAGNA

TURKEY CLUB ROULADES

Menus become elegant when you add these short-prep roulades and simple Dijon sauce.
—*Taste of Home* Test Kitchen

PREP: 20 MIN. • **COOK:** 15 MIN.
MAKES: 8 SERVINGS

- ¾ lb. fresh asparagus, trimmed
- 8 turkey breast cutlets (about 1 lb.)
- 1 Tbsp. Dijon-mayonnaise blend
- 8 slices deli ham
- 8 slices provolone cheese
- ½ tsp. poultry seasoning
- ½ tsp. pepper
- 8 bacon strips

SAUCE
- ⅔ cup Dijon-mayonnaise blend
- 4 tsp. 2% milk
- ¼ tsp. poultry seasoning

1. Bring 4 cups water to a boil in a large saucepan. Add the asparagus; cook, uncovered, 3 minutes or until crisp-tender. Drain and immediately place asparagus in ice water. Drain and pat dry. Set aside.
2. Spread turkey with Dijon-mayonnaise. Layer with the ham, provolone cheese and asparagus. Sprinkle with poultry seasoning and pepper. Roll up tightly and wrap with bacon.
3. Cook roulades in a large skillet over medium-high heat until bacon is crisp and turkey is no longer pink, turning occasionally, 12-15 minutes. Combine sauce ingredients; serve with roulades.
1 roulade with 1 Tbsp. sauce: 224 cal., 11g fat (5g sat. fat), 64mg chol., 1075mg sod., 2g carb. (1g sugars, 0 fiber), 25g pro.

NICOISE SALAD

Here's a feast for the eyes as well as the palate. The colorful garden-fresh salad is perfect with slices of crusty bread.
—Marla Fogderud, Mason, MI

PREP: 40 MIN. + COOLING
MAKES: 2 SERVINGS

- ⅓ cup olive oil
- 3 Tbsp. white wine vinegar
- 1½ tsp. Dijon mustard
- ⅛ tsp. each salt, onion powder and pepper

SALAD
- 2 small red potatoes
- ½ cup cut fresh green beans
- 3½ cups torn Bibb lettuce
- ½ cup cherry tomatoes, halved
- 10 Greek olives, pitted and halved
- 2 hard-boiled large eggs, quartered
- 1 can (5 oz.) albacore white tuna in water, drained and flaked

1. In a small bowl, whisk the oil, vinegar, mustard, salt, onion powder and pepper; set aside.
2. Place potatoes in a small saucepan and cover with water. Bring to a boil. Reduce heat; cover and simmer until tender, 15-20 minutes. Drain and cool; cut into quarters.
3. Place beans in another saucepan and cover with water. Bring to a boil. Cover and cook until crisp-tender, 3-5 minutes; drain and rinse in cold water.
4. Divide the lettuce between 2 salad plates; top with the potatoes, beans, tomatoes, olives, eggs and tuna. Drizzle with dressing.
1 serving: 613 cal., 49g fat (8g sat. fat), 242mg chol., 886mg sod., 18g carb. (3g sugars, 3g fiber), 26g pro.

NICOISE SALAD

FISH TACOS

A cool sauce with just a bit of zing perfectly tops off these crispy fish tacos. The bonus? They're not loaded with fat and calories, so I can indulge guilt-free.
—Lena Lim, Seattle, WA

PREP: 30 MIN. • **COOK:** 20 MIN.
MAKES: 8 SERVINGS

- ¾ cup reduced-fat sour cream
- 1 can (4 oz.) chopped green chiles
- 1 Tbsp. fresh cilantro leaves
- 1 Tbsp. lime juice
- 4 tilapia fillets (4 oz. each)
- ½ cup all-purpose flour
- 1 large egg white, beaten
- ½ cup panko bread crumbs
- 1 Tbsp. canola oil
- ½ tsp. salt
- ½ tsp. each white pepper, cayenne pepper and paprika
- 8 corn tortillas (6 in.), warmed
- 1 large tomato, finely chopped
  Additional fresh cilantro leaves, optional

1. Place the sour cream, chiles, cilantro and lime juice in a food processor; cover and process until blended. Set aside.
2. Cut each tilapia fillet lengthwise into 2 portions. Place the flour, egg white and panko bread crumbs in separate shallow bowls. Dip tilapia in flour, then egg white, then crumbs.
3. In a large skillet over medium heat, cook tilapia in oil in batches until fish flakes easily with a fork, 4-5 minutes on each side. Combine the seasonings; sprinkle over fish.
4. Place a portion of tilapia on each tortilla; top with about 2 Tbsp. of sour cream mixture. Sprinkle with tomato. If desired, top the tacos with additional fresh cilantro.
1 taco: 190 cal., 5g fat (1g sat. fat), 30mg chol., 269mg sod., 23g carb. (3g sugars, 2g fiber), 16g pro.
Diabetic exchanges: 2 lean meat, 1½ starch, ½ fat.

FRUITY CROISSANT PUFF

MAKE AHEAD
FRUITY CROISSANT PUFF

Here's a special breakfast recipe that came from a special friend. The tender, sweet-tart puff tastes like a berry cheese Danish.
—Myra Almer, Tuttle, ND

PREP: 10 MIN. + CHILLING
BAKE: 45 MIN. • **MAKES:** 6 SERVINGS

- 4 large croissants, cut into 1-in. cubes (about 6 cups)
- 1½ cups mixed fresh berries
- 1 pkg. (8 oz.) cream cheese, softened
- 1 cup 2% milk
- ½ cup sugar
- 2 large eggs, room temperature
- 1 tsp. vanilla extract
  Maple syrup, optional

1. Place the croissants and berries in a greased 8-in. square baking dish. In a medium bowl, beat the cream cheese until smooth. Beat in the milk, sugar, eggs and vanilla until blended; pour over the croissants. Refrigerate, covered, overnight.
2. Preheat oven to 350°. Remove the casserole from refrigerator while oven heats. Bake, covered, for 30 minutes. Bake, uncovered, until puffed and golden and a knife inserted in the center comes out clean, 15-20 minutes. Let stand for 5-10 minutes before serving. If desired, serve with syrup.
1 piece: 429 cal., 24g fat (14g sat. fat), 132mg chol., 358mg sod., 44g carb. (27g sugars, 2g fiber), 9g pro.

FISH TACOS

DENVER OMELET SALAD

Want a refreshing alternative? Toss the eggs, ham and veggies from your favorite omelet into a morning salad! It's definitely not your typical breakfast or brunch food, but it has all the right elements.
—Pauline Custer, Duluth, MN

TAKES: 25 MIN. • **MAKES:** 4 SERVINGS

- 8 cups fresh baby spinach
- 1 cup chopped tomatoes
- 2 Tbsp. olive oil, divided
- 1½ cups chopped fully cooked ham
- 1 small onion, chopped
- 1 small green pepper, chopped
- 4 large eggs
  Salt and pepper to taste

1. Arrange the spinach and tomatoes on a platter; set aside. In a large skillet, heat 1 Tbsp. olive oil over medium-high heat. Add ham, onion and green pepper; saute until ham is heated through and vegetables are tender, 5-7 minutes. Spoon over spinach and tomatoes.
2. In same skillet, heat the remaining olive oil over medium heat. Break eggs, 1 at a time, into a small cup, then gently slide into the skillet. Immediately reduce heat to low; season with salt and pepper. To prepare sunny-side up eggs, cover pan and cook until whites are completely set and yolks thicken but are not hard. Top salad with fried eggs.

1 serving: 229 cal., 14g fat (3g sat. fat), 217mg chol., 756mg sod., 7g carb. (3g sugars, 2g fiber), 20g pro.
Diabetic exchanges: 3 lean meat, 2 fat, 1 vegetable.

SHAKSHUKA BREAKFAST PIZZA

SHAKSHUKA BREAKFAST PIZZA

This distinctive pie is a spinoff of shakshuka, a classic North African and Middle Eastern dish. Its sweet, spicy and crunchy ingredients make a fun and delicious pizza.
—Phillipe Sobon, Harwood Heights, IL

PREP: 35 MIN. • **BAKE:** 15 MIN.
MAKES: 6 SERVINGS

- 1 Tbsp. olive oil
- 1 large onion, thinly sliced
- 1 Tbsp. ground cinnamon
- 1 Tbsp. paprika
- 2 tsp. ground cumin
- 2 garlic cloves, minced
- ⅛ tsp. cayenne pepper
- 1 can (14½ oz.) whole plum tomatoes, undrained
- 1 tsp. hot pepper sauce
- ½ tsp. salt
- ¼ tsp. pepper
- 1 loaf (1 lb.) frozen pizza dough, thawed
- 6 large eggs
- ½ cup crumbled feta cheese

1. Preheat oven to 400°. In a large saucepan, heat oil over medium-high heat. Add the onion; cook and stir until tender, 4-5 minutes. Add the cinnamon, paprika, cumin, garlic and cayenne; cook 1 minute longer. Stir in the tomatoes, hot pepper sauce, salt and pepper; cook and stir over medium heat until thickened, about 10 minutes.
2. Meanwhile, grease a 12-in. pizza pan. Roll the dough to fit pan. Pinch the edge to form a rim. Bake until edge is lightly browned, 10-12 minutes.
3. Spread crust with tomato mixture. Using a spoon, make 6 indentations in tomato mixture; carefully break an egg into each. Sprinkle with feta. Bake until egg whites are completely set and yolks begin to thicken but are not hard, 12-15 minutes.

1 piece: 336 cal., 12g fat (3g sat. fat), 191mg chol., 654mg sod., 41g carb. (4g sugars, 5g fiber), 16g pro.

BISCUITS & GRAVY BAKE

Traditional biscuits and gravy are usually prepared separately but served together. I baked everything in the same pan for an all-in-one casserole. Assemble it the night before, then pop it in the oven.
—Nancy McInnis, Olympia, WA

PREP: 20 MIN. + CHILLING
BAKE: 25 MIN. • **MAKES:** 10 SERVINGS

- 1   lb. bulk pork sausage
- ¼   cup all-purpose flour
- 3   cups 2% milk
- 1½ tsp. pepper
- 1   tsp. paprika
- ¼   tsp. chili powder
- 2¼ cups biscuit/baking mix
- ½   cup sour cream
- ¼   cup butter, melted

1. In a large skillet, cook the sausage over medium heat until no longer pink, 6-8 minutes, breaking into crumbles. Remove with a slotted spoon; discard drippings, reserving ¼ cup in pan. Stir in flour until blended; cook and stir until golden brown (do not burn), 1-2 minutes. Gradually whisk in milk. Bring to a boil, stirring constantly; cook and stir until thickened, 2-3 minutes. Stir in sausage, pepper, paprika and chili powder. Pour into a greased 13x9-in. baking dish. Cool completely.

2. Meanwhile, in a large bowl, mix baking mix, sour cream and melted butter until moistened. Turn onto a lightly floured surface; knead gently 8-10 times.
3. Pat or roll dough to ¾-in. thickness; cut with a floured 2½-in. biscuit cutter. Place biscuits over gravy. Refrigerate dish, covered, overnight.
4. Preheat oven to 400°. Remove the casserole from refrigerator while oven heats. Bake, uncovered, until the gravy is heated through and the biscuits are golden brown, 22-25 minutes.
Freeze option: Cover and freeze unbaked biscuits and gravy. To use, partially thaw in the refrigerator overnight. Remove from refrigerator 30 minutes before baking. Preheat the oven to 400°. Bake as directed, increasing time as needed, until gravy is heated through and biscuits are golden brown.
1 serving: 373 cal., 26g fat (11g sat. fat), 50mg chol., 640mg sod., 26g carb. (5g sugars, 1g fiber), 10g pro.

READER REVIEW
"I just prepared this for hunting camp for the second time. It won't be the last! The casserole is easy to make and has great flavor. Thanks for sharing!"
—JENNY TEPOEL, TASTEOFHOME.COM

RAMONA'S CHILAQUILES

A dear neighbor gave me her from-scratch recipe for chilaquiles. I added a few shortcuts to create a speedier version we can enjoy even when time's tight.
—Marina Castle Kelley, Canyon Country, CA

TAKES: 30 MIN. • **MAKES:** 4 SERVINGS

- ½   lb. lean ground beef (90% lean)
- ½   lb. fresh chorizo or bulk spicy pork sausage
- 1   medium onion, diced
- 1   garlic clove, minced
- 1   can (14½ oz.) diced tomatoes with mild green chiles, undrained
- 1   can (10 oz.) diced tomatoes and green chiles, undrained
- 4   cups tortilla chips (6 oz.)
- 1   cup shredded Monterey Jack cheese
     Chopped fresh cilantro
     Optional toppings: Sour cream, diced avocado and sliced red onion

1. Preheat oven to 350°. In a large skillet, cook and crumble beef and chorizo with onion and garlic over medium heat until the beef is no longer pink, 5-7 minutes; drain. Stir in both cans of tomatoes; bring to a boil.
2. In a greased 1½-qt. or 8-in. square baking dish, layer 2 cups of chips, half of the meat mixture and ½ cup cheese; repeat layers.
3. Bake until the cheese is melted, 12-15 minutes. Sprinkle with cilantro. If desired, serve with toppings.
1 serving: 573 cal., 35g fat (14g sat. fat), 110mg chol., 1509mg sod., 28g carb. (5g sugars, 4g fiber), 33g pro.

BISCUITS & GRAVY BAKE

AIR-FRYER SWEET
POTATO-CRUSTED
CHICKEN NUGGETS

AIR-FRYER SWEET POTATO-CRUSTED CHICKEN NUGGETS

Looking for a way to jazz up the usual nuggets, I tried coating them with sweet potato chips. We loved it!

—Kristina Segarra, Yonkers, NY

PREP: 15 MIN. • **COOK:** 10 MIN./BATCH
MAKES: 4 SERVINGS

- 1 cup sweet potato chips
- ¼ cup all-purpose flour
- 1 tsp. salt, divided
- ½ tsp. coarsely ground pepper
- ¼ tsp. baking powder
- 1 Tbsp. cornstarch
- 1 lb. chicken tenderloins, cut into 1½-in. pieces
  Cooking spray

1. Preheat air fryer to 400°. Place chips, flour, ½ tsp. salt, pepper and baking powder in a food processor; pulse until ground. Transfer to a shallow dish.
2. Mix cornstarch and remaining ½ tsp. salt; toss with chicken. Toss chicken with potato chip mixture, pressing to coat.
3. In batches, arrange chicken in a single layer on greased tray in air-fryer basket; spritz with cooking spray. Cook until golden brown, 3-4 minutes. Turn; spritz with cooking spray. Cook until golden brown and chicken is no longer pink, 3-4 minutes longer.

3 oz. cooked chicken: 190 cal., 4g fat (0 sat. fat), 56mg chol., 690mg sod., 13g carb. (1g sugars, 1g fiber), 28g pro.

CHICKEN POTPIE GALETTE WITH CHEDDAR-THYME CRUST

CHICKEN POTPIE GALETTE WITH CHEDDAR-THYME CRUST

This impressive galette gives classic potpie a gorgeous open-faced twist. The rich filling and flaky cheddar-flecked crust make it taste so homey and comforting.

—Elisabeth Larsen, Pleasant Grove, UT

PREP: 45 MIN. + CHILLING
BAKE: 30 MIN. + COOLING
MAKES: 8 SERVINGS

- 1¼ cups all-purpose flour
- ½ cup shredded sharp cheddar cheese
- 2 Tbsp. minced fresh thyme
- ¼ tsp. salt
- ½ cup cold butter, cubed
- ¼ cup ice water

FILLING

- 3 Tbsp. butter
- 2 large carrots, sliced
- 1 celery rib, diced
- 1 small onion, diced
- 8 oz. sliced fresh mushrooms
- 3 cups julienned Swiss chard
- 3 garlic cloves, minced
- 1 cup chicken broth
- 3 Tbsp. all-purpose flour
- ½ tsp. salt
- ¼ tsp. pepper
- 2 cups shredded cooked chicken
- ½ tsp. minced fresh oregano
- 2 Tbsp. minced fresh parsley

1. Combine flour, cheese, thyme and salt; cut in butter until crumbly. Gradually add ice water, tossing with a fork until dough holds together when pressed. Shape into a disk; refrigerate 1 hour.
2. For the filling, melt butter in a large saucepan over medium-high heat. Add carrots, celery and onion; cook and stir until slightly softened, 5-7 minutes. Add mushrooms; cook 3 minutes longer. Add the Swiss chard and minced garlic; cook until wilted, 2-3 minutes.
3. Whisk together chicken broth, flour, salt and pepper; slowly pour over the vegetables, stirring constantly. Cook until thickened, 2-3 minutes. Stir in the chicken and oregano.
4. Preheat oven to 400°. On a floured sheet of parchment, roll the dough into a 12-in. circle. Transfer to a baking sheet. Spoon the filling over the crust to within 2 in. of the edge. Fold the crust edge over the filling, pleating as you go, leaving center uncovered. Bake on a lower oven rack until the crust is golden brown and the filling is bubbly, 30-35 minutes. Cool 15 minutes before slicing. Sprinkle with minced parsley.

1 piece: 342 cal., 21g fat (12g sat. fat), 81mg chol., 594mg sod., 22g carb. (2g sugars, 2g fiber), 16g pro.

Jelly Cupboard

Homemade jams, syrups and spreads
are sure to take your brunch
right over the top.

MAKE AHEAD 5i

STRAWBERRY BUTTER

Our community has several farms where families can pick their own strawberries. We usually gather a big bucketful and can't resist sampling some in the car on the way home. But we make sure to save plenty for our berry butter!
—Kim Hammond, Watsonville, CA

PREP: 10 MIN. + CHILLING • **MAKES:** 2 CUPS

- 1 pkg. (8 oz.) cream cheese, softened
- ½ cup butter, softened
- 1 cup confectioners' sugar
- 1 tsp. vanilla extract
- 1 cup fresh strawberries, pureed

In a bowl, beat cream cheese and butter until smooth. Gradually add sugar and vanilla; mix well. Stir in the strawberries. Cover tightly and refrigerate for several hours or overnight. Store leftovers in the refrigerator up to 1 week. Serve butter with English muffins, toast, waffles or pancakes.

2 Tbsp.: 132 cal., 11g fat (7g sat. fat), 31mg chol., 100mg sod., 8g carb. (8g sugars, 0 fiber), 1g pro.

MAKE AHEAD 5i

ROSE PETAL HONEY

Brunch will be in full bloom when you set out this pretty pink honey made with rose petals. Keep it in mind for tea parties and gifts, too.
—Mary Kay Dixson, Decatur, AL

PREP: 5 MIN. • **COOK:** 35 MIN. + COOLING
MAKES: ABOUT 1 CUP

- 1 cup packed rose petals (about 6 medium roses)
- 1 cup water
- 2 Tbsp. lemon juice
- 6 Tbsp. sugar
- 1 pouch (3 oz.) liquid fruit pectin

1. In a large saucepan, combine rose petals, water and lemon juice; bring to a boil. Reduce the heat; simmer, uncovered, until petals lose their color. Strain, reserving liquid and discarding petals. Return liquid to saucepan.
2. Stir in sugar. Bring mixture to a full rolling boil over high heat, stirring constantly. Stir in fruit pectin. Continue to boil 1 minute, stirring constantly. Pour into a jar and cool to room temperature. Cover and refrigerate up to 3 weeks.

2 Tbsp.: 39 cal., 0 fat (0 sat. fat), 0 chol., 2mg sod., 10g carb. (9g sugars, 0 fiber), 0 pro.

STRAWBERRY BUTTER

HONEY CINNAMON BUTTER

Here's a simple but delectable spread for muffins and more. It's so quick to whip up, you'll want it all the time.
—Sue Seymour, Valatie, NY

TAKES: 5 MIN. • **MAKES:** ABOUT 1⅓ CUPS

- 1   cup butter, softened
- ½   cup honey
- 1   tsp. ground cinnamon

Beat all ingredients until smooth. Store, tightly covered, in the refrigerator.
1 Tbsp.: 107 cal., 9g fat (6g sat. fat), 24mg chol., 73mg sod., 7g carb. (7g sugars, 0 fiber), 0 pro.

DUTCH HONEY

I grew up on a farm, where a big, hearty breakfast was an everyday occurrence. It was a special treat when Mom served this rich syrup with our pancakes.
—Kathy Scott, Lingle, WY

TAKES: 15 MIN. • **MAKES:** 2 CUPS

- 1   cup sugar
- 1   cup corn syrup
- 1   cup heavy whipping cream
- 1   tsp. vanilla extract

In a saucepan, bring the sugar, corn syrup and heavy cream to a boil over medium heat. Cook 5 minutes or until slightly thickened, stirring occasionally. Add vanilla. Serve warm over pancakes or waffles.
2 Tbsp.: 158 cal., 6g fat (3g sat. fat), 20mg chol., 31mg sod., 29g carb. (23g sugars, 0 fiber), 0 pro.

OLD-FASHIONED FRUIT COMPOTE

OLD-FASHIONED FRUIT COMPOTE

A wonderful condiment for a holiday menu, this warm, lightly spiced fruit can simmer while you put together the rest of your meal. Or prepare the compote ahead and just reheat before serving.
—Shirley Glaab, Hattiesburg, MS

PREP: 15 MIN. • **COOK:** 1 HOUR
MAKES: 8 CUPS

- 1   can (20 oz.) pineapple chunks
- 1   can (15¼ oz.) sliced peaches
- 1   can (11 oz.) mandarin oranges
- 1   pkg. (18 oz.) pitted dried plums
- 2   pkg. (3½ oz. each) dried blueberries
- 1   pkg. (6 oz.) dried apricots
- ½   cup golden raisins
- 4   lemon zest strips
- 1   cinnamon stick (3 in.)
- 1   jar (10 oz.) maraschino cherries, drained

Drain pineapple, peaches and oranges, reserving the juices; set drained fruit aside. In a Dutch oven, combine juices, dried fruits, lemon zest and cinnamon. Bring to a boil. Reduce heat; cover and simmer until the fruit is tender, about 30 minutes. Add the canned fruit and cherries; heat through. Serve compote warm or at room temperature.
¼ cup: 126 cal., 0 fat (0 sat. fat), 0 chol., 4mg sod., 31g carb. (22g sugars, 2g fiber), 1g pro.

FRESH HERB BUTTER

I love treating my guests to flavored butter. When I mix up a big batch and store it in the freezer, I have a special spread that's ready to go whenever company arrives. Cut or pipe different shapes for extra fun.

—Pam Duncan, Summers, AR

PREP: 25 MIN. + FREEZING
MAKES: 24 SERVINGS

- 1   cup butter, softened
- 2   Tbsp. minced fresh chives
- 2   Tbsp. minced fresh parsley
- 1   Tbsp. minced fresh tarragon
- 1   Tbsp. lemon juice
- ¼   tsp. pepper

1. In a small bowl, beat all ingredients until blended. Spread the butter onto a baking sheet to ½-in. thickness. Freeze, covered, until firm.

2. Cut the butter with a 1-in. cookie cutter. Store, layered between waxed paper, in an airtight container in the refrigerator up to 1 week or in the freezer up to 3 months.

About 1 Tbsp.: 68 cal., 8g fat (5g sat. fat), 20mg chol., 61mg sod., 0 carb. (0 sugars, 0 fiber), 0 pro.

Prepare & Freeze Compound Butter

- Place the butter on a square of parchment, mounding butter into a rough log shape.

- Fold parchment toward you, enclosing the butter. Press butter with a ruler to form a log, holding the edges of the paper securely with the other hand. Twist the edges to seal. Wrap butter and freeze. Slice off the desired portions when ready to use, then rewrap the butter and return it to the freezer.

- You can also freeze scoops or rosettes of flavored butter on a parchment-lined baking sheet. Once frozen, arrange butter portions on layers of parchment paper in a freezer container. Remove the desired number of portions when needed.

FRESH HERB BUTTER

MAKE AHEAD 5i

CHRISTMAS JAM

My grandmother, a marvelous cook who really knew how to stretch a food dollar, helped inspire my passion for cooking. This cran-strawberry jam recipe is one of my favorites for the holiday season.
—Jo Talvacchia, Lanoka Harbor, NJ

PREP: 25 MIN. • **PROCESS:** 10 MIN.
MAKES: ABOUT 14 HALF-PINTS

- 1 pkg. (40 oz.) frozen unsweetened strawberries, thawed, or 2½ qt. fresh strawberries, hulled
- 1 lb. fresh or frozen cranberries, thawed
- 5 lbs. sugar
- 2 pouches (3 oz. each) liquid fruit pectin

1. Grind strawberries and cranberries in a food processor or grinder; place in a Dutch oven. Add the sugar. Bring to a full rolling boil; boil for 1 minute. Remove from the heat; stir in the pectin and return to a full rolling boil. Boil for 1 minute, stirring constantly. Remove from heat.

2. Cool for 5 minutes; skim off foam. Carefully ladle the hot mixture into hot half-pint jars, leaving ¼-in. headspace. Remove air bubbles; wipe the rims and adjust the lids. Process for 10 minutes in a boiling-water canner.

2 Tbsp.: 84 cal., 0 fat (0 sat. fat), 0 chol., 0 sod., 22g carb. (21g sugars, 0 fiber), 0 pro.

Note: The processing time listed is for altitudes of 1,000 feet or less. Add 1 minute to the processing time for each 1,000 feet of additional altitude.

PUMPKIN BUTTER

Biting into a warm biscuit topped with this fall-flavored butter is absolutely heavenly. If you added whipped cream, you just might think you were eating pumpkin pie!
—June Barrus, Springville, UT

PREP: 5 MIN. • **COOK:** 20 MIN. + COOLING
MAKES: 6 CUPS

3	cans (15 oz. each) pumpkin
2	cups sugar
1½	cups water
3	Tbsp. lemon juice
1	Tbsp. grated lemon zest
3	tsp. ground cinnamon
¾	tsp. salt
¾	tsp. ground nutmeg
¾	tsp. ground ginger

1. In a large saucepan, combine all ingredients. Bring to a boil, stirring frequently. Reduce heat; cover and simmer 20 minutes to allow flavors to blend.
2. Cool. Spoon into jars. Cover and store in the refrigerator for up to 3 weeks.
2 Tbsp.: 42 cal., 0 fat (0 sat. fat), 0 chol., 38mg sod., 11g carb. (9g sugars, 1g fiber), 0 pro.

HOMEMADE LEMON CURD

HOMEMADE LEMON CURD

Lemon curd is so scrumptious on scones and other baked goods. You can often find it next to the baking supplies or jams and jellies in larger grocery stores, but we like making it from scratch.
—Mark Hagen, Milwaukee, WI

PREP: 20 MIN. + CHILLING • **MAKES:** 1⅔ CUPS

3	large eggs
1	cup sugar
½	cup lemon juice (about 2 lemons)
¼	cup butter, cubed
1	Tbsp. grated lemon zest

In a small heavy saucepan over medium heat, whisk the eggs, sugar and lemon juice until blended. Add butter and lemon zest; cook, whisking constantly, until the mixture is thickened and coats the back of a metal spoon. Transfer to a small bowl; cool 10 minutes. Refrigerate, covered, until cold.
2 Tbsp.: 110 cal., 5g fat (3g sat. fat), 52mg chol., 45mg sod., 16g carb. (16g sugars, 0 fiber), 2g pro.

Test Lemon Curd
To know when the curd is ready, coat the back of a spoon and run your finger through it. If it leaves a path, the curd is ready. Curd will thicken slightly as it cools.

BERRY CURD

I've always loved strawberries, and it's fun to think of new uses for them when they're in season. I spoon this yummy topping over just about everything, from cake and scoops of ice cream to waffles.
—Margo Zoerner, Pleasant Prairie, WI

PREP: 5 MIN. • **COOK:** 10 MIN. + CHILLING
MAKES: ¾ CUP

- 1 cup chopped fresh strawberries
- 1 cup fresh raspberries
- ⅓ cup sugar
- 1 Tbsp. cornstarch
- 3 large egg yolks
- 2 Tbsp. butter
- 1 tsp. vanilla extract

1. Place the berries in a blender; cover and process until almost smooth. Press through a fine-mesh strainer into a bowl; reserve ½ cup plus 1 Tbsp. juice. Discard the seeds.

2. In a small heavy saucepan, mix sugar and cornstarch. Whisk in the egg yolks and berry puree until blended. Add the butter; cook over medium heat, whisking constantly, until the mixture is just thick enough to coat a metal spoon and a thermometer reads at least 170°. Do not allow to boil. Remove from heat immediately; stir in vanilla.

3. Transfer to a bowl; cool. Press plastic wrap onto surface of curd; refrigerate until cold. Serve or transfer to covered jars and refrigerate up to 2 weeks.

2 Tbsp.: 66 cal., 3g fat (2g sat. fat), 51mg chol., 18mg sod., 9g carb. (7g sugars, 1g fiber), 1g pro.

BERRY CURD

SPICED PEAR JAM

Years ago, whenever my in-laws gave me fresh pears, I canned them. Then a neighbor shared her wonderful spiced jam. It's been my go-to recipe ever since!
—Karen Bockelman, Portland, OR

PREP: 1¾ HOURS • **PROCESS:** 10 MIN.
MAKES: 6 HALF-PINTS

- 8 cups chopped or coarsely ground peeled pears (about 5½ lbs.)
- 4 cups sugar
- 1 tsp. ground cinnamon
- ¼ tsp. ground cloves

1. Combine all ingredients in a Dutch oven. Simmer, uncovered, until thick, 1½-2 hours, stirring occasionally. Stir more frequently as mixture thickens.

2. Remove from heat; skim off foam. Carefully ladle into hot half-pint jars, leaving ¼-in. headspace. Remove air bubbles; wipe rims and adjust lids. Process for 10 minutes in a boiling-water canner.

2 Tbsp.: 81 cal., 0 fat (0 sat. fat), 0 chol., 0 sod., 21g carb. (19g sugars, 1g fiber), 0 pro.

Note: The processing time listed is for altitudes of 1,000 feet or less. Add 1 minute to the processing time for each 1,000 feet of additional altitude.

The Bakery

Nothing encourages folks to linger just a little bit longer like a sweet homemade bite.

OVERNIGHT CINNAMON ROLLS

Sometimes I try different fillings in my rolls, but the cinnamon version is always a winner. They're worth the overnight wait!
—Chris O'Connell, San Antonio, TX

PREP: 35 MIN. + CHILLING
BAKE: 20 MIN. • **MAKES:** 2 DOZEN

- 2 pkg. (¼ oz. each) active dry yeast
- 1½ cups warm water (110° to 115°)
- 2 large eggs, room temperature
- ½ cup butter, softened
- ½ cup sugar
- 2 tsp. salt
- 5¾ to 6¼ cups all-purpose flour

CINNAMON FILLING
- 1 cup packed brown sugar
- 4 tsp. ground cinnamon
- ½ cup softened butter, divided

GLAZE
- 2 cups confectioners' sugar
- ¼ cup half-and-half cream
- 2 tsp. vanilla extract

1. In a small bowl, dissolve the yeast in warm water. In a large bowl, combine eggs, butter, sugar, salt, yeast mixture and 3 cups flour; beat on medium speed until smooth. Stir in enough remaining flour to form a very soft dough (dough will be sticky). Do not knead. Cover; refrigerate overnight.
2. In a small bowl, mix the brown sugar and cinnamon. Turn the dough onto a floured surface; divide the dough in half. Roll 1 portion into an 18x12-in. rectangle. Spread with ¼ cup butter to within ½ in. of edges; sprinkle the butter evenly with half of the brown sugar mixture.
3. Roll up jelly-roll style, starting with a long side; pinch seam to seal. Cut into 12 slices. Place in a greased 13x9-in. baking pan, cut side down. Repeat with the remaining dough and filling.
4. Cover with kitchen towels; let rise in a warm place until doubled, about 1 hour. Preheat oven to 375°.
5. Bake 20-25 minutes or until lightly browned. In a small bowl, mix the confectioners' sugar, cream and vanilla; spread over warm rolls.

1 roll: 278 cal., 9g fat (5g sat. fat), 39mg chol., 262mg sod., 47g carb. (23g sugars, 1g fiber), 4g pro.

5i
CHOCOLATE-DIPPED STRAWBERRY MERINGUE ROSES

Serve these lovely rose-shaped meringue cookies just as they are, or let guests crush them into individual bowls of strawberries and whipped cream. Readers of my blog went nuts when I posted that idea!
—Amy Tong, Anaheim, CA

PREP: 25 MIN. + STANDING
BAKE: 40 MIN. + COOLING • **MAKES:** 2 DOZEN

- 3 large egg whites
- ¼ cup sugar
- ¼ cup freeze-dried strawberries
- 1 pkg. (3 oz.) strawberry gelatin
- ½ tsp. vanilla extract, optional
- 1 cup 60% cacao bittersweet chocolate baking chips, melted

1. Place egg whites in a large bowl; let stand at room temperature 30 minutes. Preheat oven to 225°.
2. Place sugar and strawberries in a food processor; process until powdery. Add strawberry gelatin; pulse to blend.
3. Beat egg whites on medium speed until foamy, adding vanilla if desired. Gradually add the strawberry gelatin mixture, 1 Tbsp. at a time, beating on high after each addition until the sugar is dissolved. Continue beating until stiff glossy peaks form.
4. Cut a small hole in the tip of a pastry bag; insert a #1M star tip. Transfer the meringue to the bag. Pipe 2-in. roses 1½ in. apart onto parchment-lined baking sheets.
5. Bake 40-45 minutes or until set and dry. Turn off the oven (do not open the oven door); leave the meringues in oven 1½ hours. Remove from the oven; cool completely on baking sheets.
6. Remove the meringues from paper. Dip bottoms in melted chocolate; allow excess to drip off. Place on waxed paper; let stand until set, about 45 minutes. Store meringues in an airtight container at room temperature.

1 cookie: 33 cal., 1g fat (1g sat. fat), 0 chol., 9mg sod., 6g carb. (5g sugars, 0 fiber), 1g pro.
Diabetic exchanges: ½ starch.

READER REVIEW
"Everyone raved about these light and airy meringue treats. I piped them with the flower-decorating tip I had on hand, and the roses looked so pretty. I also spooned the chocolate on the backs of the cookies and left them chocolate side up to dry. If you like, choose a different kind of dried fruit and substitute another gelatin flavor to give these a twist."
—DUKIE1, TASTEOFHOME.COM

CHOCOLATE-DIPPED STRAWBERRY MERINGUE ROSES

ONE-BOWL CHOCOLATE CHIP BREAD

We're a family of chocoholics! When I say I'm baking this indulgent bread for breakfast, no one waits to come to the table. Plus, I don't have to rise at the crack of dawn to prepare the recipe. It calls for only five ingredients and is ready to bake in just 20 minutes.

—Angela Lively, Conroe, TX

PREP: 20 MIN. • **BAKE:** 65 MIN.
MAKES: 1 LOAF (16 PIECES)

- 3 large eggs, room temperature
- 1 cup sugar
- 2 cups sour cream
- 3 cups self-rising flour
- 2 cups semisweet chocolate chips

1. Preheat oven to 350°. Beat the eggs, sugar and sour cream until well blended. Gradually stir in flour. Fold in semisweet chocolate chips. Transfer to a greased 9x5-in. loaf pan.
2. Bake until a toothpick comes out clean, 65-75 minutes. Cool in the pan 5 minutes before removing to a wire rack to cool.

1 piece: 306 cal., 13g fat (8g sat. fat), 42mg chol., 305mg sod., 44g carb. (25g sugars, 2g fiber), 5g pro.

CINNAMON DOUGHNUT MUFFINS

CINNAMON DOUGHNUT MUFFINS

When my kids were youngsters, they loved having doughnut muffins as a treat after school or with Sunday brunch.

—Sharon Pullen, Alvinston, ON

PREP: 15 MIN. • **BAKE:** 20 MIN.
MAKES: 10 SERVINGS

- 1¾ cups all-purpose flour
- 1½ tsp. baking powder
- ½ tsp. salt
- ½ tsp. ground nutmeg
- ¼ tsp. ground cinnamon
- ¾ cups sugar
- ⅓ cup canola oil
- 1 large egg, room temperature, lightly beaten
- ¾ cup 2% milk
- 10 tsp. seedless strawberry or other jam

TOPPING
- ¼ cup butter, melted
- ⅓ cup sugar
- 1 tsp. ground cinnamon

1. In a large bowl, combine flour, baking powder, salt, nutmeg and cinnamon. In a small bowl, combine the sugar, oil, egg and milk; stir into dry ingredients just until moistened.
2. Fill greased or paper-lined muffin cups half full; place 1 tsp. jam on top. Cover the jam with enough batter to fill muffin cups three-fourths full. Bake at 350° for 20-25 minutes or until a toothpick comes out clean.
3. Place melted butter in a small bowl; combine sugar and cinnamon in another bowl. Immediately after removing the muffins from the oven, dip tops in butter, then in cinnamon sugar. Serve warm.

1 muffin: 288 cal., 13g fat (4g sat. fat), 36mg chol., 240mg sod., 40g carb. (22g sugars, 1g fiber), 4g pro.

LEMON LAYER CAKE

LEMON LAYER CAKE

Rise to the occasion with a citrusy four-layer cake topped with a luscious cream cheese frosting. The flavor, a duet of sweet and tangy notes, really sings. Lemon slices and edible flowers make the perfect decorations.
—Summer Goddard, Springfield, VA

PREP: 35 MIN. • **BAKE:** 25 MIN. + COOLING
MAKES: 12 SERVINGS

- 1 cup butter, softened
- 1½ cups sugar
- 2 large eggs, room temperature
- 3 large egg yolks, room temperature
- 1 Tbsp. grated lemon zest
- 2 Tbsp. lemon juice
- ¾ cup sour cream
- ¼ cup 2% milk
- 2½ cups all-purpose flour
- 1 tsp. salt
- 1 tsp. baking powder
- ½ tsp. baking soda

SYRUP
- ½ cup sugar
- ½ cup lemon juice

FROSTING
- 2 pkg. (8 oz. each) cream cheese, softened
- 1 cup butter, softened
- 4 cups confectioners' sugar
- 1½ tsp. lemon juice
- ⅛ tsp. salt
  Optional: Lemon slices or edible fresh flowers

1. Preheat oven to 350°. Line bottoms of 2 greased 9-in. round baking pans with parchment; grease the parchment.
2. Cream butter and sugar until light and fluffy, 5-7 minutes. Add eggs and egg yolks, 1 at a time, beating well after each addition. Beat in the lemon zest and juice. In a small bowl, mix the sour cream and milk. In another bowl, whisk together flour, salt, baking powder and baking soda; add to creamed mixture alternately with sour cream mixture.
3. Transfer to the prepared pans. Bake until a toothpick inserted in the center comes out clean, 24-28 minutes. Cool in the pans 10 minutes before removing to wire racks; remove the parchment. Cool slightly.
4. For the syrup, in a small saucepan, combine sugar and lemon juice. Bring to a boil; cook until the liquid is reduced by half. Cool completely.
5. For the frosting, beat the cream cheese and butter until smooth; beat in the confectioners' sugar, lemon juice and salt until blended.
6. Using a long serrated knife, cut each cake horizontally in half. Brush the cake layers with warm syrup; cool completely.
7. Place 1 cake layer on a serving plate; spread with 1 cup frosting. Repeat layers twice. Top with the remaining cake layer. Frost top and sides with the remaining frosting. If desired, top with lemon slices or edible flowers. Refrigerate leftovers.

1 piece: 841 cal., 48g fat (30g sat. fat), 219mg chol., 656mg sod., 96g carb. (72g sugars, 1g fiber), 8g pro.

PENNSYLVANIA DUTCH DOUGHNUTS

Mashed potatoes keep these moist, and they get a touch of sweetness from the glaze.
—Marlene Reichart, Leesport, PA

PREP: 20 MIN. + CHILLING • **COOK:** 50 MIN.
MAKES: ABOUT 4 DOZEN

- 2½ cups mashed potatoes or riced potatoes (without added milk, butter or seasonings)
- 1 cup whole milk
- 3 large eggs, room temperature, lightly beaten
- 2 Tbsp. butter, melted
- 2 cups sugar
- 2 Tbsp. baking powder
- 5 to 6 cups all-purpose flour
  Oil for deep-fat frying

GLAZE
- 2 cups confectioners' sugar
- 5 Tbsp. half-and-half cream
- ½ tsp. vanilla extract
  Optional: Food coloring and sprinkles

1. In a large bowl, combine potatoes, milk, eggs and butter. Combine sugar, baking powder and 2 cups flour; stir into potato mixture. Add enough remaining flour to form a soft dough. Refrigerate, covered, 1 hour.
2. Divide the dough in half. Turn each half onto a lightly floured surface; roll to ½-in. thickness. Cut with a 2¾-in. doughnut cutter.
3. In an electric skillet or deep-fat fryer, heat oil to 375°. Fry doughnuts, a few at a time, until golden brown on both sides. Drain on paper towels.
4. In a small bowl, mix glaze ingredients until smooth. Color the glaze if desired. Dip doughnuts in glaze and sprinkles as desired.

1 doughnut: 163 cal., 6g fat (1g sat. fat), 14mg chol., 74mg sod., 25g carb. (14g sugars, 1g fiber), 2g pro.

HOW-TO

Decorate Doughnuts

- To make decorating easy, use small bowls for different icing colors and sprinkles.

- Dip doughnuts into the glaze, and then place them on a wire rack and let them stand until set. Or dip the just-glazed doughnuts into the sprinkles.

PENNSYLVANIA DUTCH DOUGHNUTS

LEMON CHEESECAKE TARTS

Refrigerated pie crust forms the cups for these cute mini cheesecakes. Tight on time? Prepare the desserts using store-bought phyllo tart shells instead.

—Sarah Gilbert, Beaverton, OR

PREP: 30 MIN. • **BAKE:** 10 MIN. + COOLING
MAKES: 2 DOZEN

  2 **sheets refrigerated pie crust**
FILLING
  1 **pkg. (8 oz.) cream cheese, softened**
  1 **tsp. vanilla extract**
  1 **jar (10 oz.) lemon curd, divided**
  1 **container (8 oz.) frozen whipped topping, thawed**
  1 **cup fresh blueberries**
      Confectioners' sugar, optional

1. Preheat the oven to 450°. On a work surface, unroll pie crusts. Cut 24 circles with a floured 3-in. scalloped round cookie cutter, rerolling the scraps as necessary. Press the circles onto the bottoms and partway up the sides of ungreased muffin cups, smoothing the edges. Prick bottoms generously with a fork.
2. Bake until light golden brown, 5-7 minutes. Remove from the pans to wire racks to cool completely.
3. In a large bowl, beat cream cheese and vanilla until blended; beat in ¼ cup lemon curd. Fold in a third of whipped topping, then fold in remaining topping.
4. Spoon 2 Tbsp. cream cheese mixture into each tart shell; top each with 1 tsp. lemon curd. Top with berries; refrigerate until serving. If desired, sprinkle tarts with confectioners' sugar.
1 tart: 166 cal., 9g fat (5g sat. fat), 22mg chol., 95mg sod., 18g carb. (10g sugars, 0 fiber), 1g pro.

STRAWBERRY MUFFIN CONES

STRAWBERRY MUFFIN CONES

Here's a delightfully different way to serve muffins or cupcakes. Children go crazy for the ice cream look and the ease of eating from a cone. Adults can't resist either—they say that biting into one makes them feel like a kid again! Choose sprinkles that suit the holiday, season or occasion.

—Barb Kietzer, Niles, MI

PREP: 20 MIN. • **BAKE:** 20 MIN. + COOLING
MAKES: 20 SERVINGS

  2 **cups all-purpose flour**
 ½ **cup sugar**
  2 **tsp. baking powder**
 ½ **tsp. baking soda**
 ½ **tsp. salt**
  2 **large eggs, room temperature**
 ¾ **cup strawberry yogurt**
 ½ **cup canola oil**
  1 **cup chopped fresh strawberries**
 20 **ice cream cake cones (about 3 in. tall)**
  1 **cup semisweet chocolate chips**
  1 **Tbsp. shortening**
      Colored sprinkles

1. In a large bowl, combine the first 5 ingredients. In another bowl, beat the eggs, strawberry yogurt, oil and berries; stir into the dry ingredients just until moistened.
2. Place the ice cream cake cones in muffin cups; spoon 2 heaping Tbsp. batter into each ice cream cake cone. Bake at 375° for 19-21 minutes or until a toothpick inserted in the center comes out clean. Cool completely.
3. In a microwave, melt chocolate chips and shortening; stir until smooth. Dip the muffin tops in chocolate; allow excess to drip off. Decorate with sprinkles.
1 cone: 253 cal., 13g fat (3g sat. fat), 29mg chol., 196mg sod., 33g carb. (16g sugars, 1g fiber), 4g pro.

CHERRY DANISH

When I first baked a batch of these yummy from-scratch rolls for a 4-H competition years ago, I won an award. I've been baking them for friends and family ever since!
—Christie Cochran, Canyon, TX

PREP: 30 MIN. + RISING • **BAKE:** 15 MIN.
MAKES: 40 SERVINGS

- 1 pkg. (¼ oz.) active dry yeast
- ¼ cup warm water (110° to 115°)
- 1 cup warm 2% milk (110° to 115°)
- ¾ cup shortening, divided
- ⅓ cup sugar
- 3 large eggs, room temperature, divided use
- 1 tsp. salt
- ¼ tsp. each ground mace, lemon extract and vanilla extract
- 4 to 4½ cups all-purpose flour
- 1 can (21 oz.) cherry pie filling

GLAZE

- 1½ cups confectioners' sugar
- ½ tsp. vanilla extract
- 2 to 3 Tbsp. 2% milk
- ⅓ cup chopped almonds

1. In a large bowl, dissolve the yeast in warm water. Add the milk, ¼ cup shortening, sugar, 2 eggs, salt, mace, extracts and 2 cups of flour; beat until smooth. Add enough remaining flour to form a soft dough.

2. Turn onto a floured surface; knead until smooth and elastic, 6-8 minutes. Place in a greased bowl, turning once to grease top. Cover and let rise in a warm place until doubled, about 1 hour.

3. Punch dough down. On a large floured surface, roll dough out to a 24x16-in. rectangle. Dot half of dough with ¼ cup shortening; fold dough lengthwise. Fold dough 3 times lengthwise, then 2 times widthwise, each time dotting with some of remaining shortening. Place dough in a greased bowl; cover and let rise 20 minutes.

4. On a floured surface, roll the dough into a 16x15-in. rectangle. Cut into 8x¾-in. strips; coil into spiral shapes, tucking the ends underneath. Place in 2 greased 15x10x1-in. baking pans. Cover and let rise in a warm place until doubled, about 1 hour.

5. Beat the remaining egg. Make a depression in the center of each roll; brush with egg. Fill with 1 Tbsp. pie filling. Bake at 375° for 15-18 minutes or until golden brown. Cool on a wire rack. Combine the confectioners' sugar, vanilla and milk; drizzle over the rolls. Sprinkle with almonds.

1 pastry: 137 cal., 5g fat (1g sat. fat), 17mg chol., 70mg sod., 21g carb. (10g sugars, 1g fiber), 2g pro.

LEMONY WALNUT-RAISIN GALETTE

This flaky, buttery pastry has a filling of fruit, walnuts, coconut and cinnamon. There's a lot to love! For even more appeal, dollop each serving with sweetened whipped cream.
—Ellen Kozak, Milwaukee, WI

PREP: 30 MIN. • **BAKE:** 30 MIN.
MAKES: 10 SERVINGS

- 1 medium lemon
- 1 cup finely chopped walnuts
- 1 cup raisins
- 1 cup apricot spreadable fruit
- ⅔ cup unsweetened finely shredded coconut
- 2 tsp. ground cinnamon
- 8 sheets phyllo dough (14x9-in. size)
- ⅓ cup butter, melted
  Sweetened whipped cream, optional

1. Preheat oven to 350°. Cut unpeeled lemon into 8 wedges; remove seeds. Place the wedges in a food processor; process until finely chopped. Transfer to a large bowl; stir in walnuts, raisins, spreadable fruit, coconut and cinnamon.

2. Place 1 sheet of phyllo dough on a parchment-lined baking sheet; brush with butter. Layer with remaining phyllo sheets, brushing each layer. (Keep the remaining phyllo covered with a damp towel to prevent it from drying out.)

3. Spoon filling onto center of phyllo, leaving a 2-in. border on all sides. Fold the edges of phyllo over filling, leaving the center uncovered. Brush the folded edges with butter. Bake until golden brown, 30-35 minutes. Using parchment, carefully slide galette onto a wire rack to cool slightly. If desired, serve with whipped cream.

1 piece: 324 cal., 18g fat (8g sat. fat), 16mg chol., 125mg sod., 41g carb. (23g sugars, 3g fiber), 4g pro.

CHERRY DANISH

Special Menus

We've done the planning for you with 5 magnificent menus. Just add your hospitality and finishing touches.

Southern Favorites

Give guests a warm welcome with this full menu of southern-inspired brunch favorites.

QUICK AMBROSIA
FRUIT SALAD

GRITS & SAUSAGE
CASSEROLE

HOMEMADE BISCUITS
& MAPLE SAUSAGE
GRAVY

SWEET TEA
CONCENTRATE

HAM & COLLARDS
QUICHE

SWEET TEA
CONCENTRATE

SWEET TEA CONCENTRATE

Sweet iced tea is a classic southern favorite, and this concentrate is perfect for sweet-tea lovers who always like to have some on hand. Keep the recipe in mind for parties and other gatherings, too—it makes 20 servings.
—Natalie Bremson, Plantation, FL

PREP: 30 MIN. + COOLING
MAKES: 20 SERVINGS (5 CUPS CONCENTRATE)

    2 medium lemons
    4 cups sugar
    4 cups water
 1½ cups English breakfast tea leaves
       or 20 black tea bags
   ⅓ cup lemon juice
EACH SERVING
    1 cup cold water
       Ice cubes

1. Remove peels from lemons; save fruit for another use.
2. In a large saucepan, combine sugar and water. Bring to a boil over medium heat. Reduce heat; simmer, uncovered, until sugar is dissolved, 3-5 minutes, stirring occasionally. Remove from the heat; add tea leaves and lemon peels. Cover and steep for 15 minutes. Strain tea, discarding tea leaves and lemon peels; stir in the lemon juice. Cool to room temperature.
3. Transfer concentrate to a container with a tight-fitting lid. Store in the refrigerator for up to 2 weeks.
To prepare tea: In a tall glass, combine water with ¼ cup of tea concentrate; add ice.
¼ cup concentrate: 165 cal., 0 fat (0 sat. fat), 0 chol., 27mg sod., 43g carb. (40g sugars, 0 fiber), 0 pro.

GRITS & SAUSAGE CASSEROLE

GRITS & SAUSAGE CASSEROLE

You could call this the "so good casserole." That's what people say when they taste it! I love the convenience of assembling it the night before and simply popping the pan in the oven in the morning.
—Marie Poppenhager, Old Town, FL

PREP: 30 MIN. • **BAKE:** 1¼ HOURS
MAKES: 12 SERVINGS

    3 cups water
    1 cup quick-cooking grits
   ¾ tsp. salt, divided
    2 lbs. bulk pork sausage, cooked
       and drained
    2 cups shredded cheddar cheese,
       divided
    3 large eggs
 1½ cups whole milk
    2 Tbsp. butter, melted
       Pepper to taste

1. In a saucepan, bring water to a boil. Slowly whisk in grits and ½ tsp. salt. Reduce heat; cover and simmer for 5 minutes, stirring occasionally.
2. In a large bowl, combine the grits, sausage and 1½ cups cheese. Beat eggs and milk; stir into grits mixture. Add the butter, pepper and remaining salt.
3. Transfer to a greased 13x9-in. baking dish. Bake, uncovered, at 350° until a knife inserted in center comes out clean, about 1 hour. Sprinkle with the remaining cheese; bake 15 minutes longer or until cheese is melted. Let stand for 5 minutes before cutting.
Overnight option: Refrigerate unbaked casserole, covered, overnight. Remove from the refrigerator 30 minutes before baking. Bake as directed.
1 cup: 316 cal., 24g fat (11g sat. fat), 110mg chol., 621mg sod., 13g carb. (3g sugars, 1g fiber), 13g pro.

**HOMEMADE BISCUITS
& MAPLE SAUSAGE GRAVY**

HOMEMADE BISCUITS & MAPLE SAUSAGE GRAVY

I have fond memories of digging into flaky, gravy-smothered biscuits on Christmas morning and other special occasions when I was a child. What a way to start the day!
—Jenn Tidwell, Fair Oaks, CA

PREP: 30 MIN. • **BAKE:** 15 MIN.
MAKES: 8 SERVINGS

- 2   cups all-purpose flour
- 3   tsp. baking powder
- 1   Tbsp. sugar
- 1   tsp. salt
- ¼   tsp. pepper, optional
- 3   Tbsp. cold butter, cubed
- 1   Tbsp. shortening
- ¾   cup 2% milk

SAUSAGE GRAVY
- 1   lb. bulk maple pork sausage
- ¼   cup all-purpose flour
- 3   cups 2% milk
- 2   Tbsp. maple syrup
- ½   tsp. salt
- ¼   tsp. ground sage
- ¼   tsp. coarsely ground pepper

1. Preheat oven to 400°. In a large bowl, whisk the flour, baking powder, sugar, salt and, if desired, pepper. Cut in cold butter and shortening until the mixture resembles coarse crumbs. Add milk; stir just until moistened. Turn onto a lightly floured surface; knead gently 8-10 times.

2. Pat or roll dough to 1-in. thickness; cut with a floured 2-in. biscuit cutter. Place biscuits 1 in. apart on an ungreased baking sheet. Bake until golden brown, 15-17 minutes.

3. Meanwhile, in a large skillet, cook the pork sausage over medium heat until no longer pink, 6-8 minutes, breaking into crumbles. Stir in the flour until blended; gradually stir in milk. Bring to a boil, stirring constantly; cook and stir until sauce is thickened, 4-6 minutes. Stir in the remaining ingredients. Serve gravy with warm biscuits.

1 biscuit with ½ cup gravy: 371 cal., 19g fat (8g sat. fat), 41mg chol., 915mg sod., 38g carb. (11g sugars, 1g fiber), 11g pro.

HAM & COLLARDS QUICHE

Quiche is one of my breakfast favorites. When I wanted something that celebrates my southern roots, I came up with this recipe. The eggs, cheese, ham and collard greens make every slice a complete meal.
—Billie Williams-Henderson, Bowie, MD

PREP: 20 MIN. • **BAKE:** 35 MIN. + STANDING
MAKES: 6 SERVINGS

- 1 sheet refrigerated pie crust
- 2 Tbsp. olive oil
- 1 cup frozen chopped collard greens, thawed and drained
- 1 small onion, chopped
- 1 garlic clove, minced
- ¼ tsp. salt
- ¼ tsp. pepper
- 2 cups shredded Colby-Monterey Jack cheese
- ¾ cup cubed fully cooked ham
- 6 large eggs
- 1 cup 2% milk

1. Preheat oven to 375°. Unroll crust into a 9-in. pie plate; flute edge. Chill while preparing filling.

2. In a large skillet, heat the oil over medium-high heat. Add collard greens and onion; cook and stir until the onion is tender, 5-7 minutes. Add garlic; cook 1 minute longer. Stir in salt and pepper. Cool slightly; stir in cheese and ham. Spoon into crust.

3. In a large bowl, whisk the eggs and milk until blended. Pour over the top. Bake on lower oven rack until a knife inserted in the center comes out clean, 35-40 minutes. Cover edge loosely with foil during the last 15 minutes if needed to prevent overbrowning. Remove foil. Let stand 10 minutes before cutting.

Freeze option: Cover and freeze unbaked quiche. To use, remove from the freezer 30 minutes before baking (do not thaw). Preheat the oven to 375°. Place quiche on a baking sheet. Bake as directed, increasing time to 50-60 minutes.

1 piece: 457 cal., 31g fat (15g sat. fat), 240mg chol., 766mg sod., 23g carb. (4g sugars, 1g fiber), 21g pro.

QUICK AMBROSIA FRUIT SALAD

You've gotta love a 10-minute brunch dish! It leaves a lot of time to devote to the rest of the menu. I mix in a little coconut and just enough marshmallows so my salad tastes like the creamy ambrosia I grew up with.
—Trisha Kruse, Eagle, ID

TAKES: 10 MIN. • **MAKES:** 6 SERVINGS

- 1 can (8¼ oz.) fruit cocktail, drained
- 1 can (8 oz.) unsweetened pineapple chunks, drained
- 1 cup green grapes
- 1 cup seedless red grapes
- 1 cup miniature marshmallows
- 1 medium banana, sliced
- ¾ cup vanilla yogurt
- ½ cup sweetened shredded coconut

In a large bowl, combine all of the ingredients. Chill until serving.

¾ cup: 191 cal., 4g fat (3g sat. fat), 2mg chol., 48mg sod., 40g carb. (34g sugars, 2g fiber), 3g pro.

HAM & COLLARDS QUICHE

Easter Brunch

Celebrate with Easter classics:
glazed ham, roasted asparagus
and pretty pastel sweets.

EASTER EGG BREAD

I've made this Easter treat for 20 years! Colored hard-cooked eggs baked into the dough give the braided loaf such a festive look for the holiday. Leave them out, and the recipe can be enjoyed anytime. My husband especially likes this sweet bread with ham.
—Heather Durante, Wellsburg, WV

PREP: 55 MIN. + RISING
BAKE: 25 MIN. + COOLING
MAKES: 1 LOAF (16 PIECES)

½ cup sugar
2 pkg. (¼ oz. each) active dry yeast
1 to 2 tsp. ground cardamom
1 tsp. salt
6 to 6½ cups all-purpose flour
1½ cups whole milk
6 Tbsp. butter, cubed
4 large eggs, room temperature, divided use
3 to 6 hard-boiled large eggs, unpeeled
  Assorted food coloring
  Canola oil
2 Tbsp. water

1. In a large bowl, mix sugar, yeast, cardamom, salt and 2 cups flour. In a small saucepan, heat milk and butter to 120°-130°. Add to the dry ingredients; beat on medium speed 2 minutes. Add 3 eggs; beat on high 2 minutes. Stir in enough remaining flour to form a soft dough (dough will be sticky).

2. Turn dough onto a floured surface; knead 6-8 minutes or until smooth and elastic. Place dough in a greased bowl, turning once to grease top. Cover and let rise in a warm place until doubled, about 45 minutes.

3. Meanwhile, dye the hard-boiled eggs with food coloring following package directions. Let stand until completely dry.

4. Punch down dough. Turn onto a lightly floured surface; divide into thirds. Roll each portion into a 24-in. rope. Place ropes on a greased baking sheet and braid. Bring the ends together to form a ring. Pinch ends to seal. Lightly coat dyed eggs with oil; arrange on braid, tucking them gently among the ropes.

5. Cover with a kitchen towel; let rise in a warm place until doubled, about 20 minutes. Preheat the oven to 375°.

6. In a bowl, whisk the remaining egg and water; gently brush over dough, avoiding eggs. Bake 25-30 minutes or until golden brown. Remove from pan to a wire rack to cool. Refrigerate leftovers.

1 piece: 281 cal., 8g fat (4g sat. fat), 107mg chol., 231mg sod., 44g carb. (8g sugars, 1g fiber), 9g pro.

READER REVIEW
"This dyed-egg loaf is absolutely gorgeous, and everyone loved it. I highly recommend the recipe! We did have some left over, and I can't wait to make French toast casserole with the extra bread."
—DANIELLEYLEE, TASTEOFHOME.COM

**APRICOT GINGER
MUSTARD-GLAZED HAM**

APRICOT GINGER MUSTARD-GLAZED HAM

One year, I tried baking my holiday ham with a sweet-and-spicy ginger glaze. It made our special-occasion meal even more special.
—Ally Phillips, Murrells Inlet, SC

PREP: 15 MIN. • **BAKE:** 2 HOURS
MAKES: 16 SERVINGS

- 1 fully cooked bone-in ham (7 to 9 lbs.)
- ½ cup drained canned apricot halves
- ½ cup stone-ground mustard
- ⅓ cup packed brown sugar
- 2 Tbsp. grated fresh gingerroot
- 1 Tbsp. whole peppercorns
- ½ tsp. sea salt
- ½ tsp. coarsely ground pepper

1. Preheat oven to 325°. Place ham on a rack in a shallow roasting pan. Using a sharp knife, score surface of ham with ¼-in.-deep cuts in a diamond pattern. Cover and bake until a thermometer reads 130°, 1¾-2¼ hours.
2. Meanwhile, place the remaining ingredients in a food processor; process until blended.
3. Remove ham from oven. Increase oven setting to 425°. Spread apricot mixture over the ham. Bake the ham, uncovered, until a thermometer reads 140°, 15-20 minutes longer. If desired, increase oven setting to broil; broil until golden brown, 2-4 minutes.
4 oz. cooked ham: 201 cal., 6g fat (2g sat. fat), 87mg chol., 1258mg sod., 8g carb. (7g sugars, 0 fiber), 30g pro.

ROASTED ASPARAGUS WITH THYME

Here's a classic way to welcome spring to your table. The light, simply seasoned asparagus is easy to prepare yet elegant.
—Sharon Leno, Keansburg, NJ

TAKES: 20 MIN. • **MAKES:** 12 SERVINGS

- 3 lbs. fresh asparagus, trimmed
- 3 Tbsp. olive oil
- 2 tsp. minced fresh thyme or ¾ tsp. dried thyme
- ½ tsp. salt
- ¼ tsp. pepper

1. Place asparagus in a baking pan lined with heavy-duty foil. Drizzle with oil and toss to coat. Sprinkle with the thyme, salt and pepper.

ROASTED ASPARAGUS WITH THYME

2. Bake, uncovered, at 425° until crisp-tender, 10-15 minutes.
7 spears: 55 cal., 4g fat (1g sat. fat), 0 chol., 101mg sod., 4g carb. (0 sugars, 1g fiber), 3g pro.
Diabetic exchanges: 1 vegetable, ½ fat.

ONION-GARLIC HASH BROWNS

A tasty potato medley with slow-cooker convenience, this recipe is a go-to side dish. Stir in a bit of hot sauce if you like some heat, or sprinkle your finished hash browns with a little shredded cheddar cheese.
—Cindi Boger, Ardmore, AL

PREP: 20 MIN. • **COOK:** 3 HOURS
MAKES: 12 SERVINGS

- ¼ cup butter, cubed
- 1 Tbsp. olive oil
- 1 large red onion, chopped
- 1 small sweet red pepper, chopped
- 1 small green pepper, chopped
- 4 garlic cloves, minced
- 1 pkg. (30 oz.) frozen shredded hash brown potatoes
- ½ tsp. salt
- ½ tsp. pepper
- 3 drops hot pepper sauce, optional
- 2 tsp. minced fresh parsley

1. In a large skillet, heat the butter and oil over medium heat. Add the onion and peppers. Cook and stir until crisp-tender. Add garlic; cook 1 minute longer. Stir in hash browns, salt, pepper and, if desired, hot pepper sauce.
2. Transfer to a 5-qt. slow cooker coated with cooking spray. Cook, covered, until heated through, 3-4 hours. Sprinkle with parsley just before serving.
½ cup: 110 cal., 5g fat (3g sat. fat), 10mg chol., 136mg sod., 15g carb. (1g sugars, 1g fiber), 2g pro.
Diabetic exchanges: 1 starch, 1 fat.

**LEMON PUDDING
DESSERT**

LEMON PUDDING DESSERT

*After a big feast, people really go for this
sunny lemon dessert. I've prepared it for
church suppers for years, and I always get
recipe requests. The shortbread crust is the
perfect base for the fluffy layers of cream
cheese, pudding and whipped topping.*
—Muriel DeWitt, Maynard, MA

PREP: 20 MIN. + CHILLING
BAKE: 20 MIN. • **MAKES:** 16 SERVINGS

- 1 cup cold butter, cubed
- 2 cups all-purpose flour
- 1 pkg. (8 oz.) cream cheese, softened
- 1 cup confectioners' sugar
- 1 carton (8 oz.) frozen whipped
  topping, thawed, divided
- 3 cups cold whole milk
- 2 pkg. (3.4 oz. each) instant lemon
  pudding mix

1. Preheat oven to 350°. Cut the butter
into the flour until crumbly. Press into
an ungreased 13x9-in. baking dish. Bake
until light brown, 18-22 minutes. Cool
on a wire rack.

2. Beat cream cheese and sugar until
smooth. Fold in 1 cup whipped topping.
Spread over cooled crust.
3. Beat milk and pudding mix on low
speed for 2 minutes. Carefully spread
over cream cheese layer. Top with the
remaining whipped topping. Refrigerate
at least 1 hour.
1 piece: 348 cal., 20g fat (13g sat. fat), 49mg
chol., 305mg sod., 35g carb. (22g sugars,
0 fiber), 4g pro.

🄵 BIRD NESTS

*My kids love helping me build fun little
nests of sweet coated pretzels topped
with Peeps chicks and chocolate eggs.*
—Jessica Boivin, Nekoosa, WI

PREP: 40 MIN. • **MAKES:** 2 DOZEN

- 2 pkg. (10 to 12 oz. each) white baking
  chips
- 1 pkg. (10 oz.) pretzel sticks
- 24 yellow chicks Peeps candy
- 1 pkg. (12 oz.) M&M's eggs or other
  egg-shaped candy

1. In a large metal bowl set over a pot of
simmering water, melt the baking chips;
stir until smooth. Reserve ½ cup melted
chips for decorations; keep warm.
2. Add pretzel sticks to remaining chips;
stir to coat evenly. Drop the mixture into
24 mounds on waxed paper; shape into
bird nests using 2 forks.
3. Dip the bottoms of Peeps in reserved
chips; place in nests. Attach eggs with
remaining chips. Let stand until set.
1 nest: 276 cal., 11g fat (7g sat. fat), 7mg
chol., 215mg sod., 41g carb. (30g sugars,
1g fiber), 4g pro.

READER REVIEW
*"I assembled these cute edible
nests with my 7-year-old sister,
and she had a blast making and
eating them. They couldn't have
been easier or yummier!"*
—DOBYLOVER2008, TASTEOFHOME.COM

BIRD NESTS

Pancake & Waffle Buffet

Fire up the griddle, get your batter ready
and let the creativity begin.

THE BEST EVER
PANCAKES

OVERNIGHT
YEAST WAFFLES

THE BEST EVER PANCAKES

It's no exaggeration when I say I make pancakes every weekend! I crave them in any form and variation, but these from-scratch cakes just can't be beat.
—James Schend, Pleasant Prairie, WI

PREP: 15 MIN. • **COOK:** 5 MIN./BATCH
MAKES: 4 SERVINGS

1½ cups all-purpose flour
2 Tbsp. sugar
1 tsp. baking powder
½ tsp. baking soda
½ tsp. salt
1 cup buttermilk
2 large eggs, room temperature
¼ cup butter, melted

1 tsp. vanilla extract
Optional: Mixed fresh berries, whipped cream, maple syrup and butter

1. In a large bowl, whisk together the first 5 ingredients. In another bowl, whisk remaining ingredients; stir into dry ingredients just until moistened.
2. Preheat griddle over medium heat. Lightly grease griddle. Pour batter by ¼ cupfuls onto the griddle; cook until bubbles on top begin to pop and bottoms are golden brown. Turn; cook until the second side is golden brown. Serve with toppings as desired.

3 pancakes: 360 cal., 15g fat (8g sat. fat), 126mg chol., 817mg sod., 45g carb. (10g sugars, 1g fiber), 10g pro.

THE BEST EVER PANCAKES

Make a Great Pancake Bar

What's the secret to setting up the perfect pancake and waffle bar? Provide lots of options! Here are ideas to get you started.

Spreads
- Butter
- Peanut butter
- Nutella
- Marshmallow fluff
- Jam or preserves
- Pie filling
- Yogurt
- Lemon curd

Toppings
- Fresh fruits: blueberries, strawberries or bananas
- Toasted nuts
- Shredded sweetened coconut
- Sprinkles
- Mini chocolate chips
- Mini marshmallows
- Granola
- Dried fruit: cherries or cranberries
- Crumbled cooked bacon

Finishing Touches
- Honey
- Maple syrup
- Caramel sauce
- Chocolate sauce
- Whipped cream
- Cinnamon sugar

OVERNIGHT
YEAST WAFFLES

5i
HOME FRIES

When I was a girl, my dad and I would get up before everyone else on Sundays and prepare these bacon-flavored potatoes for the family. The aroma got sleepyheads rushing to the table!
—Teresa Koide, Manchester, CT

PREP: 25 MIN. • **COOK:** 15 MIN./BATCH.
MAKES: 8 SERVINGS

- 1 lb. bacon, chopped
- 8 medium potatoes (about 3 lbs.), peeled and cut into ½-in. pieces
- 1 large onion, chopped
- 1 tsp. salt
- ½ tsp. pepper

1. In a large skillet, cook the chopped bacon over medium-low heat until crisp. Remove the bacon from the pan with slotted spoon and drain on paper towels. Remove the bacon drippings from pan and reserve.
2. Working in batches, add ¼ cup bacon drippings, the potatoes, onion, salt and pepper to pan; toss to coat. Cook and stir over medium-low heat until potatoes are golden brown and tender, 15-20 minutes, adding more drippings as needed. Stir in cooked bacon; serve immediately.
1 cup: 349 cal., 21g fat (8g sat. fat), 33mg chol., 681mg sod., 31g carb. (3g sugars, 2g fiber), 10g pro.

MAKE AHEAD
OVERNIGHT YEAST WAFFLES

With batter you whip up the night before and store in the fridge, homemade waffles are just moments away in the morning.
—Mary Balcomb, Florence, OR

PREP: 15 MIN. + CHILLING
COOK: 5 MIN./BATCH • **MAKES:** 10 SERVINGS

- 1 pkg. (¼ oz.) active dry yeast
- ½ cup warm water (110° to 115°)
- 1 tsp. sugar
- 2 cups warm 2% milk (110° to 115°)
- ½ cup butter, melted
- 2 large eggs, room temperature
- 2¾ cups all-purpose flour
- 1 tsp. salt
- ½ tsp. baking soda

1. In a large bowl, dissolve yeast in warm water. Add sugar; let stand for 5 minutes. Add the milk, butter and eggs; mix well. Combine the flour and salt; stir into milk mixture. Cover and refrigerate overnight.
2. Stir the batter; add baking soda and stir well. Bake waffles in a preheated waffle iron according to manufacturer's directions until golden brown.
2 waffles: 220 cal., 12g fat (7g sat. fat), 74mg chol., 366mg sod., 22g carb. (3g sugars, 1g fiber), 6g pro.

HOW-TO
DIY Waffle Sliders
Cook waffle batter by heaping tablespoonfuls in the waffle iron. Make sandwiches with whipped cream, berries or other toppers.

CHOCOLATE LOVER'S PANCAKES

These indulgent pancakes are light and fluffy, with a rich but not-too-sweet flavor from the cocoa. They're fantastic topped with either maple or chocolate syrup—and even better with both swirled together!
—Harland Johns, Leesburg, TX

PREP: 15 MIN. • **COOK:** 5 MIN./BATCH
MAKES: 4 SERVINGS

- 1   cup all-purpose flour
- ¼   cup baking cocoa
- 2   Tbsp. sugar
- 1   tsp. baking powder
- ½   tsp. baking soda
- ½   tsp. salt
- 1   cup buttermilk
- 1   large egg, room temperature
- 2   Tbsp. butter, melted
- 1   tsp. vanilla extract
     Maple syrup and chocolate syrup

1. In a large bowl, whisk flour, cocoa, sugar, baking powder, baking soda and salt. In another bowl, whisk buttermilk, egg, melted butter and vanilla until blended. Add to dry ingredients and stir just until moistened.

2. Place a greased large nonstick skillet over medium heat. In batches, pour the batter by ¼ cupfuls onto the skillet; cook until the bubbles on top begin to pop and the bottoms are golden brown. Turn; cook until second side is golden brown. Serve with syrups.

2 pancakes: 271 cal., 8g fat (4g sat. fat), 64mg chol., 753mg sod., 42g carb. (16g sugars, 2g fiber), 8g pro.

CHOCOLATE LOVER'S PANCAKES

TROPICAL BERRY SMOOTHIES

TROPICAL BERRY SMOOTHIES

The best smoothies taste like a treat while delivering a nutritious boost to your day. A blend of pina colada juice, berries, yogurt and mango, this recipe appeals to kids and adults alike. It's also easy to increase based on the number of people you'll be serving.
—Hillary Engler, Cape Girardeau, MO

TAKES: 10 MIN. • **MAKES:** 2 SERVINGS

1 cup pina colada juice blend
1 container (6 oz.) vanilla yogurt
⅓ cup frozen unsweetened strawberries
¼ cup frozen mango chunks
¼ cup frozen unsweetened blueberries

In a blender, combine all ingredients; cover and process for 30 seconds or until smooth. Pour into chilled glasses; serve immediately.
1¼ cups: 172 cal., 2g fat (1g sat. fat), 4mg chol., 62mg sod., 35g carb. (32g sugars, 2g fiber), 5g pro.

Oatmeal & Smoothie Bar

Bowl guests over with wholesome, nutritious smoothie bowls and hearty oats with customizable toppings.

FRUIT SMOOTHIE BOWLS

RAISIN NUT
OATMEAL

LIME COCONUT
SMOOTHIE BOWL

SLOW-COOKER
COCONUT GRANOLA

LIME COCONUT
SMOOTHIE BOWL

This eaten-by-the-spoonful smoothie is like a tropical breeze—the most refreshing thing on the planet! Mango, pineapple and more blend for a taste of paradise.
—Madeline Butler, Denver, CO

TAKES: 15 MIN. • **MAKES:** 2 SERVINGS

- 1 medium banana, peeled and frozen
- 1 cup fresh baby spinach
- ½ cup ice cubes
- ½ cup cubed fresh pineapple
- ½ cup chopped peeled mango or frozen mango chunks
- ½ cup plain Greek yogurt
- ¼ cup sweetened shredded coconut
- 3 Tbsp. honey
- 2 tsp. grated lime zest
- 1 tsp. lime juice
- ½ tsp. vanilla extract
- 1 Tbsp. spreadable cream cheese, optional
  Optional: Lime wedges, sliced banana, sliced almonds, granola, dark chocolate chips and additional shredded coconut

Place first 11 ingredients in a blender; if desired, add cream cheese. Cover and process until smooth. Pour into chilled bowls. Serve immediately, with optional toppings as desired.
1 cup: 325 cal., 10g fat (7g sat. fat), 15mg chol., 80mg sod., 60g carb. (51g sugars, 4g fiber), 4g pro.

SLOW-COOKER
COCONUT GRANOLA

When you see how easy it can be to make granola, you'll never want the store-bought kind again. Replace the cherries with other dried fruits for a twist.
—*Taste of Home* Test Kitchen

PREP: 15 MIN. • **COOK:** 3½ HOURS
MAKES: 12 SERVINGS

- 4 cups old-fashioned oats
- 1 cup sliced almonds
- 1 cup unsweetened coconut flakes
- 1 tsp. ground cinnamon
- 1 tsp. ground ginger
- ¼ tsp. salt
- ½ cup coconut oil, melted
- ½ cup maple syrup
- 1 cup dried cherries

1. Combine the oats, almonds, coconut, cinnamon, ginger and salt in a 3-qt. slow cooker. In small bowl, whisk together oil and maple syrup. Pour into slow cooker; stir to combine. Cook, covered, on low, stirring occasionally, 3½-4 hours. Stir in cherries.
2. Transfer the mixture to a baking sheet; let stand until cool.
½ cup: 343 cal., 19g fat (12g sat. fat), 0 chol., 55mg sod., 41g carb. (18g sugars, 5g fiber), 6g pro.

MAKE AHEAD
RAISIN NUT OATMEAL

What better way to wake up than to a hot, ready-to-eat breakfast? This comforting oatmeal simmers away while you sleep and gives you a morning treat.
—Valerie Sauber, Adelanto, CA

PREP: 10 MIN. • **COOK:** 7 HOURS
MAKES: 6 SERVINGS

- 3½ cups fat-free milk
- 1 large apple, peeled and chopped
- ¾ cup steel-cut oats
- ¾ cup raisins
- 3 Tbsp. brown sugar
- 4½ tsp. butter, melted
- ¾ tsp. ground cinnamon
- ½ tsp. salt
- ¼ cup chopped pecans

In a 3-qt. slow cooker coated with cooking spray, combine the first 8 ingredients. Cover and cook on low for 7-8 hours or until liquid is absorbed. Spoon the oatmeal into bowls; sprinkle with pecans.
¾ cup: 289 cal., 9g fat (3g sat. fat), 10mg chol., 282mg sod., 47g carb. (28g sugars, 4g fiber), 9g pro.

READER REVIEW
"I love overnight oatmeal! This is a great recipe, and the nicest thing is that you can change the add-ins if you want."
—333MELLO333, TASTEOFHOME.COM

SWEET
KAHLUA
COFFEE

SWEET KAHLUA COFFEE

Want to perk up your java? With Kahlua, creme de cacao and a dollop of whipped cream, the usual cup of coffee turns into a perfectly indulgent treat.
—Ruth Gruchow, Yorba Linda, CA

PREP: 10 MIN. • **COOK:** 3 HOURS
MAKES: 8 SERVINGS (ABOUT 2 QT.)

- 2   qt. hot water
- ½   cup Kahlua (coffee liqueur)
- ¼   cup creme de cacao
- 3   Tbsp. instant coffee granules
- 2   cups heavy whipping cream
- ¼   cup sugar
- 1   tsp. vanilla extract
- 2   Tbsp. grated semisweet chocolate

1. In a 4-qt. slow cooker, mix the water, Kahlua, creme de cacao and instant coffee granules. Cook, covered, on low 3-4 hours or until heated through.
2. In a large bowl, beat heavy whipping cream until it begins to thicken. Add the sugar and vanilla; beat until soft peaks form. Serve warm coffee with whipped cream and chocolate.
1 cup: 337 cal., 23g fat (15g sat. fat), 68mg chol.,19mg sod., 21g carb. (18g sugars, 0 fiber), 2g pro.

FRUIT SMOOTHIE BOWLS

Smoothie bowls give an instant boost to any brunch buffet. They're easy to make, fun to eat and totally customizable with all sorts of flavorful toppings.
—*Taste of Home* Test Kitchen

TAKES: 15 MIN. • **MAKES:** 6 SERVINGS

- 2½ cups 2% milk
- 2   cups frozen unsweetened sliced peaches
- 2   cups frozen unsweetened strawberries
- ½   cup orange juice
- ¼   cup honey
     Optional toppings: Fresh berries, chia seeds, pumpkin seeds, flaxseed and toasted chopped nuts

In a blender, combine half of the milk, peaches, strawberries, juice and honey; cover and process until smooth. Transfer to a large pitcher. Repeat, adding the second batch to the same pitcher; stir to combine. Serve immediately. Add toppings as desired.
1 cup: 140 cal., 2g fat (1g sat. fat), 8mg chol., 49mg sod., 27g carb. (24g sugars, 2g fiber), 4g pro.

OVERNIGHT FLAX OATMEAL

Fans of the healthy benefits of flaxseed will love this hearty oatmeal full of raisins and dried cranberries. Many substitutions will work as well, so feel free to get creative!
—Susan Smith, Ocean View, NJ

PREP: 10 MIN. • **COOK:** 7 HOURS
MAKES: 4 SERVINGS

- 3   cups water
- 1   cup old-fashioned oats
- 1   cup raisins
- ½   cup dried cranberries
- ½   cup ground flaxseed
- ½   cup 2% milk
- 1   tsp. vanilla extract
- 1   tsp. molasses
     Optional: Sliced almonds, whole milk and additional molasses

In a 3-qt. slow cooker, combine all ingredients. Cover and cook on low for 7-8 hours or until the liquid is absorbed and the oatmeal is tender. If desired, top with sliced almonds, whole milk and additional molasses.
1 cup: 322 cal., 9g fat (1g sat. fat), 2mg chol., 28mg sod., 63g carb. (34g sugars, 8g fiber), 9g pro.

OVERNIGHT
FLAX OATMEAL

Christmas Morning Feast

A leisurely brunch makes a fabulous present. Check it off your list with this marvelous make-ahead menu.

THREE-CHEESE QUICHE

CHRISTMAS MORNING
SWEET ROLLS

FESTIVE
CRANBERRY
FRUIT SALAD

MONTE CRISTO CASSEROLE WITH RASPBERRY SAUCE

MAKE AHEAD

MONTE CRISTO CASSEROLE WITH RASPBERRY SAUCE

My husband's a fan of the classic ham and cheese sandwich, the Monte Cristo. I experimented with the basic recipe and created a baked casserole. It's a terrific variation to serve for brunch.
—Mary Steiner, Parkville, MD

PREP: 20 MIN. + CHILLING
BAKE: 30 MIN. + STANDING
MAKES: 10 SERVINGS (1¾ CUPS SAUCE)

- 1   loaf (1 lb.) French bread, cut into 20 slices
- 2   Tbsp. Dijon mustard
- ½   lb. sliced deli ham
- ½   lb. sliced Swiss cheese
- ½   lb. sliced deli turkey
- 6   large eggs
- 1½ cups whole milk
- 2   tsp. sugar
- 2   tsp. vanilla extract

TOPPING
- ½   cup packed brown sugar
- ¼   cup butter, softened
- ½   tsp. ground cinnamon

RASPBERRY SAUCE
- ⅓   cup sugar
- 1   Tbsp. cornstarch
- ¼   cup cold water
- ¼   cup lemon juice
- ¼   cup maple syrup
- 2   cups fresh or frozen raspberries

1. Line a greased 13x9-in. baking dish with half the bread. Spread mustard over bread. Layer with ham, cheese, turkey and remaining bread (dish will be full).
2. In a large bowl, whisk the eggs, milk, sugar and vanilla; pour over the top. Refrigerate, covered, overnight.
3. Preheat oven to 375°. Remove the casserole from refrigerator while oven heats. In a small bowl, mix the topping ingredients; sprinkle over casserole. Bake, uncovered, until golden brown, 30-40 minutes.
4. Meanwhile, in a small saucepan, combine sugar and cornstarch. Stir in cold water, lemon juice and syrup until smooth. Add raspberries. Bring to a boil; cook and stir until thickened, about 2 minutes. Cool sauce slightly.
5. Let casserole stand 10 minutes before cutting. Serve with sauce.
1 piece with about 3 Tbsp. sauce: 476 cal., 17g fat (8g sat. fat), 167mg chol., 906mg sod., 55g carb. (29g sugars, 3g fiber), 25g pro.

FESTIVE CRANBERRY FRUIT SALAD

THREE-CHEESE QUICHE

Eggs and cheese are at their best in this easy yet special crustless quiche. My guests often mention how tall, light and fluffy it is, and no one misses the crust.
—Judy Reagan, Hannibal, MO

PREP: 15 MIN. • **BAKE:** 45 MIN. + STANDING
MAKES: 6 SERVINGS

- 7 large eggs
- 5 large egg yolks
- 1 cup heavy whipping cream
- 1 cup half-and-half cream
- 1 cup shredded part-skim mozzarella cheese
- ¾ cup shredded sharp cheddar cheese, divided
- ½ cup shredded Swiss cheese
- 2 Tbsp. finely chopped oil-packed sun-dried tomatoes
- 1½ tsp. salt-free seasoning blend
- ¼ tsp. dried basil

1. Preheat oven to 350°. In a large bowl, combine the eggs, egg yolks, whipping cream, half-and-half cream, mozzarella cheese, ½ cup cheddar cheese, Swiss cheese, tomatoes, seasoning blend and basil; pour into a greased 9-in. deep-dish pie plate. Sprinkle with the remaining cheddar cheese.
2. Bake 45-50 minutes or until a knife inserted in the center comes out clean. Let stand 10 minutes before cutting.
1 piece: 449 cal., 37g fat (21g sat. fat), 524mg chol., 316mg sod., 5g carb. (3g sugars, 0 fiber), 22g pro.

FESTIVE CRANBERRY FRUIT SALAD

A tradition on my Christmas table, this tangy fruit bowl comes together quickly—a big plus on such an eventful day!
—Rousheen Arel Wolf, Delta Junction, AK

TAKES: 25 MIN. • **MAKES:** 14 SERVINGS

- 1 pkg. (12 oz.) fresh or frozen cranberries
- ¾ cup water
- ½ cup sugar
- 5 medium apples, diced
- 2 medium firm bananas, sliced
- 1½ cups fresh or frozen blueberries, thawed
- 1 can (11 oz.) mandarin oranges, undrained
- 1 cup fresh or frozen raspberries, thawed
- ¾ cup fresh strawberries, halved

1. In a large saucepan, combine the cranberries, water and sugar. Cook and stir over medium heat until berries pop, about 15 minutes. Remove from heat; cool slightly.
2. In a large bowl, combine the remaining ingredients. Add the cranberry mixture; stir gently. Refrigerate until serving.
¾ cup: 105 cal., 0 fat (0 sat. fat), 0 chol., 2mg sod., 27g carb. (21g sugars, 4g fiber), 1g pro.

CHRISTMAS
MORNING
SWEET ROLLS

CHRISTMAS MORNING SWEET ROLLS

These homemade treats have been a holiday staple for years. The eggnog in the frosting is an extra special touch for the season.
—Kimberly Williams, Brownsburg, IN

PREP: 45 MIN. + CHILLING
BAKE: 20 MIN. • **MAKES:** 1 DOZEN

- 1 pkg. (¼ oz.) active dry yeast
- 1 cup warm water (110° to 115°)
- ½ cup sugar
- 1 tsp. salt
- 4 to 4½ cups all-purpose flour
- ¼ cup canola oil
- 1 large egg, room temperature

FILLING
- ⅓ cup sugar
- 1½ tsp. ground cinnamon
- ¼ tsp. ground nutmeg
- 3 Tbsp. butter, softened

FROSTING
- 2½ cups confectioners' sugar
- 5 Tbsp. butter, softened
- ½ tsp. ground cinnamon
- ½ tsp. vanilla extract
- 2 to 3 Tbsp. eggnog

1. In a small bowl, dissolve the yeast in warm water. In a large bowl, combine sugar, salt, 1 cup flour, oil, egg and the yeast mixture; beat on medium speed until smooth. Stir in enough remaining flour to form a soft dough (dough will be sticky).
2. Do not knead. Place in a greased bowl, turning once to grease the top. Cover and refrigerate overnight.
3. For the filling, in a small bowl, mix sugar, cinnamon and nutmeg. Punch down dough; turn onto a lightly floured surface. Roll into an 18x8-in. rectangle. Spread with the butter to within ½ in. of the edges; sprinkle with the sugar mixture. Roll up jelly-roll style, starting with a long side; pinch the seam to seal. Cut into 12 slices.
4. Place the slices in a greased 13x9-in. baking pan, cut side down. Cover with a kitchen towel; let rise in a warm place until doubled, about 45 minutes.
5. Preheat oven to 350°. Bake rolls until golden brown, 20-25 minutes. Place pan on a wire rack. Beat confectioners' sugar, butter, cinnamon, vanilla and enough eggnog to reach desired consistency; spread over warm rolls.
1 roll: 424 cal., 13g fat (5g sat. fat), 37mg chol., 267mg sod., 72g carb. (39g sugars, 2g fiber), 5g pro.

MAKE-AHEAD EGGS BENEDICT TOAST CUPS

5i

MAKE-AHEAD EGGS BENEDICT TOAST CUPS

When I was growing up, our family always had eggs Benedict with champagne and orange juice for Christmas breakfast. Now I'm cooking, and I made the meal a little easier by creating these delicious cups.
—Lyndsay Wells, Ladysmith, BC

PREP: 30 MIN. • **BAKE:** 10 MIN.
MAKES: 1 DOZEN

- 6 English muffins, split
- 1 envelope hollandaise sauce mix
- 12 slices Canadian bacon, quartered
- 1 tsp. pepper
- 1 Tbsp. olive oil
- 6 large eggs
- 1 Tbsp. butter

1. Preheat oven to 375°. Flatten English muffin halves with a rolling pin; press into greased muffin cups. Bake until lightly browned, about 10 minutes.
2. Meanwhile, prepare the hollandaise sauce according to package directions; cool slightly. Sprinkle the bacon with pepper. In a large skillet, cook bacon in oil over medium heat until partially cooked but not crisp. Remove to paper towels to drain. Divide bacon among muffin cups. Wipe skillet clean.
3. Whisk the eggs and ½ cup cooled hollandaise sauce until blended. In the same skillet, heat butter over medium heat. Pour in egg mixture; cook and stir until eggs are thickened and no liquid egg remains. Divide egg mixture among muffin cups; top with remaining sauce. Bake until heated through, 8-10 minutes.
Overnight option: Refrigerate unbaked cups, covered, overnight. Bake until the cups are golden brown, 10-12 minutes.
Freeze option: Cover and freeze the unbaked cups in muffin cups until firm. Transfer to an airtight container; return to the freezer. To use, bake the cups in muffin tin as directed, increasing time to 25-30 minutes. Cover cups loosely with foil if needed to prevent overbrowning.
1 toast cup: 199 cal., 11g fat (5g sat. fat), 114mg chol., 495mg sod., 15g carb. (2g sugars, 1g fiber), 9g pro.

INDEX